To San[illegible]r
Cruz and Mother

God Works Miracles

Stenson E Tolan

By

Stenson Edward Tolan JR

Copyright

Dedication

To my beloved mother, Margaret Shaw Tolan, and my beautiful wife, Lois Tolan. Also, Cousin Eddie Tolan (Track and Field Athlete), Cousin Jessie Owens (Track and Field Athlete), Brother Bobby Tolan (Professional Baseball Player), Eric Uyeno, Ty McKinley Ranger, Danny Smart (Santa Monica Police), Sergeant Luna (Sheriff), Audrey Miranda, Isaiah Miranda, Juana Miranda, Fernando Miranda, Gerardo Miranda, Jennifer Miranda, Vanessa Miranda, and Jerry Miranda.

Acknowledgment

I thank all the people, especially my brother Stanley, who motivated me to expose the ill-treatment toward senior citizens, whether it was in the form of encouragement or resentment.

Contents

Chapter 1: Life...

Everyone has aspirations and dreams that define us and set us apart from the crowd. Mine is simple: be good to others and hope the same to be returned to me. But life...it never goes as one aspires it to be. There's always something that startles life's boat and sends us convulsing at different periods of our lives. Perhaps the tragic turn of events has made me this bitter and, perhaps, even non-comprehensible for many. So, allow me to narrate my story from the start.

Ever since I was a boy, I wanted to create an impact. I wanted to be successful in life, I wanted people to recognize my efforts, and I wanted to do good to the people. It was simple again: do good and receive good. Or perhaps, I was too naïve.

As a young boy, my first job was cutting grass and mowing lawns. Although many people would consider this job boring, I never missed a day because I believed it to be my moral responsibility, and how could I not mention the satisfaction I got after receiving my allowance. It was as if my hard work was returned to me in another form—in currency papers stamped from my blood and sweat. I loved every bit of the process.

Every sphere of my life reflects my ideology of working hard and helping and lifting others. My work record shows my dedication to creating a difference and my now personal life...well, that is a story that is burdening my heart the moment I'm documenting my voice.

It was not all bad in the beginning. As I mentioned earlier, life's boat convulses at different periods, and not at all times.

My family life as a child had its ups and downs. My mother divorced my father, and my custody was given to her. She raised me well and taught me to be resilient toward life. Although I was grieving the loss of a split family, my mother showed me an optimistic angle to an otherwise devastating situation, and I am forever thankful to her for this act of kindness.

In my adolescent years, I met the love of my life. She was the girl whose smile could defeat a thousand rainbows. Her eyes glistened with wisdom, and her face was the most angelic one I had ever seen. I fell for her—hard. The commotion in my heart could not stay concealed for long, for I professed my love for her.

She was startled. She did not expect such a bold move from anyone, let alone the most handsome guy from her class (her words, not mine).

Well, she accepted my proposal, which marked the beginning of my love affair. She was my everything, and soon I made that official by sliding the ring into her delicate finger.

I vividly remember the day. Her walk down the aisle. The contentment in her eyes. And the exchange of our vows. Everything was perfect and magical.

We started our lives together and multiplied from two to four in a span of some years. I became a father to a boy and to a girl who were so dear to me. I could see my reflection embodied in their faces; they were a part of me.

My wife made our home a sweet haven, and her motherly instincts were always way ahead of my paternal affection. She knew what was best for her children, and I am glad that I fully supported her endeavors.

Sometimes, the kids treated their mother irrationally, and that would upset my loving wife. In such circumstances, I recalled the struggles my mother went through to raise me. Needless to say, the memories, even though blurred, resonated a sad hymn, which iterated my mother's hardships even more before my eyes. Thus, whenever I spotted kids being harsh to their mother, I would always reprimand them. "You only get one mother, so you should respect her," I would say, and perhaps these words were to accredit my own mother's hard work.

Life ran on its course, and we succeeded in building a supportive relationship within our family. Until came the hurricane in my life…the loss of my dear wife.

It was a fine morning, and everything was following the routine. I went to check up on my wife, and there she was, seated on the chair with her hands clasping her head. Her eyes were closed, and she was squealing with pain. Seeing such a disturbing picture, I asked: "Are you alright, dear?"

"Yes, just a headache, I think." My wife informed me without opening her eyes.

"Well, it certainly does not appear so. Let's take you to the hospital," I responded worryingly, as I spotted her grinding her teeth as an involuntary action to the pain.

"No…I just need some rest, that's all." Despite her downplaying, I forced her to go to the hospital with me. She was the mother of my children, after all. My love interest. My wife! I could not let her be; I could not let her sob in pain alone.

As we reached the hospital, my wife had a stroke then and there. It bothers me to date that none of the hospital staff stepped up to attend to a woman in such a condition. I was the one who had to usher my wife to the emergency while controlling my own throbbing emotions.

Life was never the same after this unfortunate event, and my wife then needed someone to look after her. So, I became her shadow I used to feed her, take her on walks, and, of course, to the beauty shop. In fact, I enjoyed doing all of this for my wife, for her giggles were the biggest return I could ask for.

I lost the precious soul in 2010, which marked an end to the beautiful era of my life. To this day, I miss her, and I wish she were here with me. But then again, I wish the opposite because she would be devastated to see me in this condition.

Before we get into details, let me brief you about my children. I wanted my kids to follow my suit, so I tried to instill the same habits in my children. I taught them to work hard and do good to the people around them. But did I succeed here?

I'm shaking as I write this—no! They failed to adopt any manners I tried to teach them. They forgot the lessons I preached about kindness and goodwill because they were too tempted to replace priceless emotions with material objects. But how do I know? It is because they did wrong to none but their own father!

I had a loving relationship with both my kids until they became materialistic. Sure, we had some good times together, but those memories became worthless as soon as they stabbed me in the back. I can't put into words how much they disappointed me. All I wanted from them was good morals and the return...oh, well.

I had bought a house in 1977 with my hard-earned money, whose each room was bricked with my devotion and commitment to raising a supportive and loving family. This house, I believed, was to be my home post-retirement. But my son made sure that none of it happens.

Despite all my efforts, Stenson Edward Tolan (III) did not work hard in life, and since a family's job is to support others in need, I let him stay with me in my house. Little did I know that my own blood curdled and snatched my property from me, leaving me in my senior years homeless and lonely.

I went to my daughter for support, and I was certain that she would help me on the matter. I was crushed; not only she refused to help me, but she also told me that I should let go of my property. To her, Stenson Edward Tolan (III) was young and the future rightful heir of the property. Hence, creating an issue on the matter was insignificant in her eyes.

The irony is that I fathered these children, and I always told them to do good to others. My life's boat was anchored and crushed on the shore—by my own children who did not even respect my age.

Interestingly, my life aspiration, as I am writing this, has not yet faltered. I still want to do good to others, which is why I am penning my experience in this book; I do not want others to face the same consequences as I did. So, please read my story and fill yourself with the information to safeguard yourself from the dire aftermath that I encountered.

Chapter 2: The Payback

My aspirations in life were of a simplistic man. So, when I purchased the house in 1977, I thought I established a foundation that could sustain my good days. I saw a home where I could spend some quality time with my wife in my retirement years. I envisaged a happy beginning with an elated end. But I envisioned all that, only to be disappointed.

Besides my wife crossing the bridge, my son made sure that every dream I had in my eyes was snatched, crushed, and forgone. No, I'm not a bitter person, and no, I'm not writing this story to gain sympathy or pity. All I want is to document hundreds of thousands of people whose voice is suppressed. I want to speak for those who lost their entire life savings to such circumstances. I want to stand for senior citizens who are easy to manipulate and taken advantage of. I want all of these people to know that they are not alone and that there must be a solution to all this malice going in our lives.

So, how exactly did I lose my house and other belongings? Let me explain in as intelligible way as possible.

It all started when my son moved into my house because he was jobless and needed my support to sustain his lifestyle. I welcomed him with open arms; after all, that's what family does.

To those implying that he was a grown-up man and that I should have shut him out—yes, probably you are right, but, as I said, I am a simple man. He is my blood, and no father wants to see his kid suffer through life's ordeals. I had to shelter him, and that I did.

But perhaps my son over welcomed his stay. He invited his girlfriend, Taby Mason, to stay over, and I must say that's when the real distortion of my life picture took place.

Let me fill you up on Taby first. The girl is very smart, dangerously cunny, and her mother is no different. The mother-daughter couple has some goals in life, and from what I've deciphered, some of them are power control, money hoarding, and destroying my life.

Why am I putting these allegations on them? Well, I have enough reason, and let me tell you why. My son acquired a job at Dr. Murphy's clinic, where Pat Mason—Taby's mother—was the supervisor. Dr. Murphy was our consultant doctor, and as per medical procedures, my wife—when she was alive—and I were bound to share our personal information. Of course, the Dr. and his associates were required to keep our confidential information confined to medical procedures; however, they did not.

Taby Mason had all the information I had provided to the clinic, and she used that to her benefit. This right here is a violation of the HIPPA Privacy Rule, which I will discuss at length in the upcoming chapters. For now, let me tell you the anguishing tale of becoming homeless.

When Taby moved in, she tried to lure me into believing that she was looking after me. She was hotheaded—I must say—and very outspoken to charm anyone in her bounds. Well, good for her, but she used this ability to maneuver her moves and deprive me of my home.

One fine day, I went out to run some errands. I took on the bus and witnessed the freshness in the air. I thought that my life was coming together despite the highs and lows I was accustomed to. I missed my wife terribly that day, but I felt like a piece of me was ready to transit into other roles—perhaps a grandpa one day. I was daydreaming, which maybe people my age usually do.

I don't know how I got things done that day, but I was glad that I was home...please excuse my digression; I just was really hurt at this point.

So, when I returned home, I was astonished to find that all the door locks were changed. My medicines, my clothes, my accessories...everything was locked inside and away from me. I, the owner, was standing outside the front door, banging and requesting others to open the door for me. There was no response, and I felt as if I was once again mourning my loss. My hopes came tumbling down, and this time, I felt defeated.

Nobody can fight death, and when my wife left my side, I knew that it was beyond my control. Despite that, I mourned for years because that was a tragic loss. My house, on the other hand, was still something I could fight back, or so I thought.

Still, tears left my eyes this time because my perception of a happy life was once again challenged. I sat outside the house for hours that I can't even calculate; my back hurt, my throat parched, and my eyes got rheumy. I waited and waited until I figured that sitting around with my silhouette won't buy me any favors and that I should ask relevant authorities to hand me my house back. But what happened next…I was not ready for it.

I went to every legal institution where I was subject to further abuse by the so-called 'protectors.' I tried, over and over again, to explain my situation, but it all fell on deaf ears. I only got as far as: "Why did you sign the papers?"

Okay, allow me to explain myself here. There are two possibilities of transferring my house papers to the Los Angeles County Assessor's Office. First: I signed the papers some time back and placed them in my study. Later my son and his girlfriend stole them to serve their purpose. Second: they went through my paperwork and forged my signature. In either case, I did not submit the papers or sign the notary book. So, do you see the tyranny in the above-asked question?

Even if we assume that one of these conditions is true, I have numerous questions that nobody to date has answered.

The first and foremost being, why did the Los Angeles County Assessor's Office did not contact me after receiving the Preliminary Change of Ownership Report form?

The form clearly states that "your telephone number and/or email address is very important. If there is a question or a problem, the Assessor needs to be able to contact you." So, why was this point neglected?

All of the involved people owe me an explanation to these concerns of mine:

- On what grounds did the office officiate the property transfer?
- Why did they not ask for an I.D.?
- Is that justified for anyone to go through; especially, the senior citizens?

All the devil's works need devil's advocates to go to succession. And in my case, the devil is my son, and his advocates are Taby Mason, Pat Mason, Dr. Murphy (from the dental office), and the so-called fair system.

I have been battling this 'enterprise' for some time, and in the chapters ahead, I will name every involved person and explain how and why they became part of the process. Also, let's dissect this matter with an objective eye so that you can help me and others to reclaim their 'lifetime investments.'

Tragically, the senior citizens are the most at risk through these loopholes in the system, and it is about time that relevant authorities help us restore what's truly ours.

Chapter 3: The Mist in the Fog

We are told that this world is a balance between right and wrong. So, if you are on the suffering side of the scale, you must believe that someone can help you there.

When it comes to injustice, we count on law enforcement agencies to counter our problems. We think that they have our back, and no matter the gravity of the situation, these departments will continue to serve us.

Do you still believe so? If yes, then let me tell you that such was never the case for me. I pleaded for help from every department concerning my case, but nobody believed me, and some even looted money from me. I, an elderly man, was left to succumb to this treatment with no remorse.

I went from department to department, asking for help, telling them that my lifetime investment is taken away because of their negligence, but they spare me no ears. So, here I am, warning others who are going through the same ordeal…nobody will help you.

When I found out that my house was no longer mine, it was hard to fathom. I mean, I did not sign the notary book or showed my I.D. to the respective department. So, naturally, I was confused about the property transfer process.

To comb this tangled mess, I went to the accessor's office and asked for an explanation. I was given none and was told "You should not have signed the papers." Again, I expounded on the matter that I did not sign anything, and that was the whole point of me paying them a visit.

Disappointed, I went to Los Angeles Police Department (LAPD) to seek justice. I made my way to the reception desk, where I met Delph (batch number: 36375). She did not pay heed to my concerns, and I felt as if asking for justice was a crime. I think that people on the front desk should not be as rigid as she was because that only adds up to the frustration and desperation level of the suffering ones.

Then I went to Detective Casalicchzo (batch number: 37621). He did not want to hear my story and dismissed me as if I had nothing significant to buy his attention. Again, why work in the field when you are incapable of serving others?

Next came my encounter with Detective Aguirre (batch number: 4323786543), whose time again was much precious than helping me. Well, at least, he introduced me to Officer Ferman, who, after listening to my case, gave me the number: 3237865512.

Finally, a ray of hope for me, but it was soon crushed when I did not hear back from Ferman. To date, I have zero ideas why Ferman did not get back to me. So, all in all, these detectives did me no good, and I found myself back to square one.

Is this the standard working procedure for LAPD? Well, I looked up online and found information that says otherwise. It mentions that any supervisor receiving a complaint—via telephone, in person, or any written statement—must comply with the following measures.

- Investigate the case preliminarily, according to the guidelines provided in Complaint Investigations: A Guide for Supervisors.
- Fill in the complaint form and summarize the complainant's input in the summary section.
- Record all investigative interviews. In case doing so is impractical, the supervisor must include written jurisdiction in the complaint form.
- Provide the complaint form's copy to the complainant and brief them about the upcoming mail copy with the assigned case number.
- Try to resolve the case up to the complainant's satisfaction.
- Guage complainant's willingness to participate in Alternative Complaint Resolution (ACR), if eligible.
- Submit complaint form and conducted investigation report to the watch commander or section OIC.

Despite being elated reading this, I was sad because I knew firsthand that none of these guidelines were followed. My time at the police station was nothing but sheer torture, and I felt the repercussions in the many nights that followed.

Apr 01 21, 19:58 p.1

Forgery & [redacted] Illegal lockout

5/28/19 10:40 am

Rec [redacted] Filmed up LG, committed by son 77th Burglary (323) 786-5411

1201: 12805-001
1508: 12AH01-060

Elder Abuse
(323) 786-5512

Detective Aguirre
77th Burglary
(323) 786-5411

8/23/19 940

35832@LAPD.ONLINE

If you wish to comment on the level of service you received, please contact a Department supervisor or telephone (888) 374-4665, or TTY for the hearing-impaired (213) 485-3004.

I could not sleep, thinking about what had become of our police department. I am elderly, the most vulnerable of the citizens, and if these detectives were reluctant to help me, it boggles my mind considering the sufferings of others.

However, despite my hunchback and weak knees, I decided to visit Consumer Affairs Department. After all, I had invested my blood and sweat into the house, and I could not fathom the unfair treatment. I was determined to fight for my property, for my memories with my wife lingered around that place.

I met Rudy at the Consumer Affairs, and he examined all my paperwork. Meanwhile, I sat there anxiously, waiting for him to help me retrieve my former property. Every twitch of his brow and facial muscles fell heavy on my nerves. I wanted my emotional turmoil to end. I was desperate, and I needed his support.

After going through the paperwork, Rudy just said, "Why did you sign the paperwork?" With a sigh, I repeated the stance that I did not, and neither did I sign the notary book.

I recalled what I read on the Department of Consumer Affairs (DCA) website: "DCA educates consumers by giving them the information they need to avoid being victimized by unscrupulous or unqualified people who promote deceptive or unsafe services."

I expected this level of commitment from Rudy, but his smirk and a sly smile said it all. So, I gathered all my material without uttering a single word while holding my tears back and headed to the second floor. There, I met Charles from Investigative Property Division . I repeated my story, but, alas, he did not help me, too.

I was crushed beyond words. I did not know who to turn to or what to do. Nobody was paying attention to my case, and I was getting restless with every passing day. By now, I concluded that the involved departments could not help me and that I should go to Karen Bass for help. So, I did.

At her office, I was told to hire an attorney to represent my case in court. I complied with the request and hired Damian (Santa Monica Attorney), who charged me $3000 as a service fee. Since I was desperate, I paid this hefty amount and prayed for the matter to resolve.

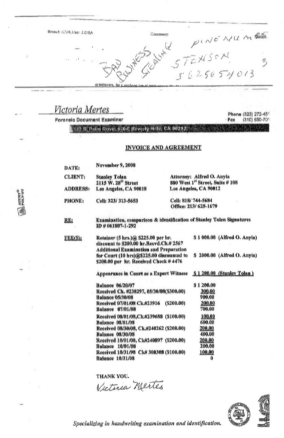

Branch :CU4,User :LOSA Comment:

BAD BUSINESS STEALING PHONE NUMBER STEHSON 5625654013

Victoria Mertes
Forensic Document Examiner
Phone (323) 272-451
Fax (310) 650-701
137 S. Palm Drive, #304 Beverly Hills, CA 90212

INVOICE AND AGREEMENT

DATE: November 9, 2008

CLIENT: Stanley Tolan
2115 W. 28th Street
ADDRESS: Los Angeles, CA 90018

Attorney: Alfred O. Anyia
880 West 1st Street, Suite # 108
Los Angeles, CA 90012

PHONE: Cell: 323/ 313-5653

Cell: 818/ 744-5684
Office: 213/ 625-1679

RE: Examination, comparison & identification of Stanley Tolen Signatures
ID # 061807-1-292

FEE(S):

Retainer (5 hrs.)@ $225.00 per hr. discount to $200.00 hr.Recvd.Ck.# 2567	$ 1 000.00 (Alfred O. Anyia)
Additional Examination and Preparation for Court (10 hrs)@$225.00 discounted to $200.00 per hr. Received Check # 4476	$ 2000.00 (Alfred O. Anyia)
Appearance in Court as a Expert Witness	$ 1 200.00 (Stanley Tolan)
Balance 06/20/07	$ 1 200.00
Received Ck. #238297, 05/30/08($300.00)	300.00
Balance 05/30/08	900.00
Received 07/01/08 Ck.#23916 ($200.00)	200.00
Balance 07/01/08	700.00
Received 08/01/08,Ck.#239688 ($100.00)	100.00
Balance 08/01/08	600.00
Received 08/30/08, Ck.#240262 ($200.00)	200.00
Balance 08/30/08	400.00
Received 10/01/08, Ck#240897 ($200.00)	200.00
Balance 10/01/08	200.00
Received 10/31/98 Ck# 300308 ($100.00)	100.00
Balance 10/31/08	0

THANK YOU.

Victoria Mertes

Specializing in handwriting examination and identification.

As a result of this hire, my son and his girlfriend sued me, and Dr. Murphy helped them with the lawyer. This created a Statute of Limitation—the maximum period during which the parties having a dispute must initiate legal procedures. Well, my attorney failed me and told me to hire someone other than him.

Damian said, "I know that the son and his girlfriend stole your house. I know it, but I can do no nothing about it."

These words hit me like a hammer. I had already lost my house, and then on top of that I paid this guy a handsome amount from my pocket and what for? To receive this statement?

It was hard for me, but I discarded the idea of proceeding justice through court because of this very reason. My next course was asking social workers for help, so I went to Ridley Thomas and explained my situation at the Civil Rights Meeting. I was really hopeful about this, given that the attendees were top-notch supervisors who could help me with my case. For the most part, they cross-questioned me and saw me through the dubious lens. Perhaps, they did not want to believe me.

Thomas assigned my case to a social worker, but it was futile because that led to nowhere. So, this closed the chapter of seeking justice through supervisors.

My voice is suppressed, and I am stranded in my elderly years. Despite so much struggle, I am unable to seek justice for myself, and the legal system has failed me. This experience has made me realize the adversity a senior citizen goes through in America, and I am deeply aggrieved at this sad state .

We have given our precious years to the country, and we at least deserve justice from the concerned institutions. This is our age to benefit from the assets we have lawfully made over the years. But we are receiving quite the opposite treatment.

The question is: how to change such a legal setup? Well, the change initiates with us, and you need to realize that you, my readers, can help people like me receive justice. So, please read through this information carefully and avoid these channels where justice is clogged.

Another reason for writing this book is to explain the ordeal I went through: elder abuse, violation of HIPPA Law, forgery, and illegal lockout. So, read on and save yourself and your loved ones from such heinous offenses.

Chapter 4: Work Like a Trojan

I had been homeless in my senior years, and one might perceive that my son had done enough damage and injustice to me. But that was not all. His greedy nature, fueled by his girlfriend's encouragement, weaved many disastrous plans for my survival.

So, if you believe I have faced the worst adversity possible, wait until I tell you what he did further. For him, snatching my home from me was apparently not enough. So, along with his girlfriend, he went through my paperwork again to rip me off further. The devil designs of their mind gave them two different options: selling my car along with other belongings and acquiring a loan on my residential property.

Both options served their materialistic approach, perhaps the reason why they decided to pursue each of them. But was it justified to do to an old man, who posed them no harm? Was it an acceptable attitude for a senior citizen who sheltered them in their devastating times? There is no justification that validates their heinous attempt at making money from my belongings.

First, they changed the locks to my personal residence to limit my access. Okay, I get it. They wanted the house, and they did. But what they did next was beyond my apprehension—they did not shy away from garnering money by selling my belongings. If you think that nothing can stoop below this level…well, wait until I tell you more.

First off, they sold my 75 Pontiac to literally the next person they saw, the junk man. Think about my feelings at this instant. Of course, I didn't learn about this move until later, but I was gutted as soon as I learned. All my hard work seemed gushing away into the non-existent dimension.

Since I was shattered beyond repair, I decided to confront my son on the matter, but before I could do that, another news hit me hard on the head. My son, with the help of his girlfriend, Taby Mason, used my paperwork and went to Bank of America for a loan application. *They'll never get it* should be everyone's initial thought, but what if I tell you it was quite the contrary.

Soon, I learned that Stenson Edward Tolan (III) and Taby got a total of $60,000 from the bank. This news came as a shock, and I decided to meet Patricia, Taby's mother, for clarity. The mother told me that the couple didn't plan to pay the loan back, putting my property at risk. Of course, I panicked and went to the bank to bring this turn of events to their notice. One thing was on my mind: how did the bank accept his application?

In fact, I learned about the loan because it was lent in my name to my son. Naturally, I was confused about how the bank mortgaged my property to someone else without my consent.

I filed my complaint and waited for a response from their end. Sure, the bank did contact me, and its customer service representatives left their voice mails, but did they make any difference to my situation? Not really! And it was because they didn't listen to me and I felt berated explaining myself every now and then.

I was faced with the same question: why did I sign the papers? I iterated again and again that I did not; otherwise, I would never have come to them for help. I always believed that the customer service of this institution is immaculate, but unfortunately, my experience did not resonate well with this belief. The people at the bank blatantly rejected my complaint and told me that I was unreasonable.

People question me what I did to retrieve my lost property and money in such dire conditions. Well, remember I hired a lawyer? Yes, I lost more money paying him for his services—the one that didn't get me anywhere. So, I lost the initial money with this surplus altogether.

Now, my house is in Stenson Edward Tolan's (III) name, from which he has made substantial money by acquiring the loan. He has also added to his riches by selling my personal belongings, including my car.

Meanwhile, I, a senior citizen, am asking authorities to help me with my case. And since the plea is falling on deaf ears, I believe educating the citizens about this dilemma is the ultimate solution.

In the following chapter, I will explain all the violated laws and their implications in detail. So, read them and decide for yourself: is this how we want to treat our senior citizens?

Chapter 5: Blind to Justice

I have knocked on the door of every institution in Los Angeles for justice, and I have spent numerous dollars acquiring the services of lawyers and attorneys, yet I haven't gotten anywhere. Not that my case is weak...no, that's not the reason derailing my justice. It is the relevant personnel's ignorance toward my case that I find myself helpless.

When I narrated my story, I promised you that I would explain what went wrong in detail. Since, by now, I have mentioned my son's wrongdoings, I will now discuss the bypassed laws to give you a complete picture of the situation.

A number of laws were bypassed, for which I have also registered my complaint against them, as mentioned in chapter three. So, what exactly are these charges, and how were they levied? Let me enlighten you about those now.

HIPAA Privacy Rule

The Health Insurance Portability and Accountability Act of 1996 (HIPAA), a federal law, mandates the protection of sensitive patient data from being disclosed without the patient's knowledge or consent. To preserve information, including but not limited to patient's health, national standards are created by the U.S. Department of Health and Human Services (HHS).

The HIPAA Privacy Rule addresses the disclosure of protected health information by organizations/individuals—known as 'covered entities'—subjected to the rule.'

The main idea behind this privacy rule is to discourage the use of sensitive information while permitting the flow of health information required to receive quality health care. In simple words, HIPAA Privacy Rule restricts the use of patient information in matters other than health care and among people other than medical professionals.

According to the HHS.gov website, individually identifiable health information includes the following.

- The individual's past, present, and future health and conditions.
- The facilities or provisions utilized by the patient.
- The past, present, or future payment made by the patient to the health care units for provisions.

Such information can leak a patient's private credentials/data, and that is exactly what happened to me at Dr. Murphy's Dental Office. The doctor misused my information and passed it on to his associates for reasons unbeknownst to me. I mean, I was ripped off from my own house, and my mental condition was deterred because of Dr. Murphy's negligence. Whether this information leak was deliberate or not, it is an open violation of the HIPPA Law, and Dr. Murphy's Dental Office must pay for their mishap.

Elder Abuse

According to California Penal Code Section 368 (g), an elder is a person aged 65 years or more. Since this age bracket is frail and deficient at taking care of themselves, they are easy targets to abuse.

This abuse can be emotional, physical, financial, and even sexual in some instances. Unfortunately, I fell victim to the former three types; let me explain how.

Emotional Elder Abuse

My son and his girlfriend caused me emotional and psychological distress by yelling at me and intimidating me. I have recordings of Taby yelling at me with "you should be ashamed of yourself" being her favorite go-to line.

Of course, living with an abuser 24/7 has its consequences, and I felt utterly dejected from life. Their hurtful dialogs are still etched in my memory, and if that is not emotional elder abuse, I don't know what is.

Physical Elder Abuse

Physical abuse refers to non-accidental use of force against a senior citizen, resulting in an injury, impairment, or physical discomfort. When Stenson Edward Tolan (The Third) and Taby Mason locked me out of my own house, I was uncomfortable. I did not have access to my personal belongings, and that was devastating. Furthermore, I was restrained from accessing my medicine which further added to my discomfort.

Financial Elder Abuse

This type of abuse refers to unauthorized utilization of elder's resources, funds, or properties. Well, my son and his partner are guilty of using all these elements without my consent, and thus, they are an accomplice to financial abusers.

According to Penal Code Section 368, the following must be done to prove the person(s) guilty.

- Establish that the said person(s) inflicted physical discomfort or mental distress to an elderly.
- Prove that the said person(s) acted willfully with criminal negligence.
- Provide evidence that the said person(s) knew that their harm was inflicted on an elder (65 years or older).
- Verify that the said person(s) acted under circumstances that were likely to produce physical pain, bodily injury, or death.

Since I can prove all of these, Stenson Edward Tolan (The Third) and Taby Mason are guilty of a felony, and they must be punished accordingly.

Secondly, Bank of America acted as an accomplice to the couple's evil plans. Thus, the bank shares the blame and is equally responsible for financially abusing me.

Forgery

According to Penal Code 470, forgery is defined as doing any of the following activities with the motive to commit fraud:

- Falsifying or changing the contents of a legal document.
- Forging signatures of others.
- Recreating another person's handwriting.
- Faking a falsified document as genuine.

When I was locked out of my house, Taby assisted my son to forge documents and mail them without my consent to the accessor's department. They both are old enough to know that this was an unethical act, yet knowingly, they proceeded.

Penal Code 470 Conviction penalties are severe and are totally dependent on the prosecutor's discretion to convict one with a misdemeanor or felony. Generally, this decision is based on an individual's criminal record.

If convicted of a misdemeanor, the individual may be punished with a fine of up to $1,000, one year in county jail, informal probation, and/or restitution for the victims.

If convicted of a felony, the individual may be punished with a fine of up to $10,000, up to three years in jail, formal probation, and/or restitution to the victims.

I rest the case to the concerned authorities to determine if my son and her partner committed a misdemeanor or a felony and request them to take action accordingly.

Illegal Lockout

In California, it is illegal to change locks, and even the landlord cannot do so in the presence of tenants. Otherwise, the landlord is liable to pay fines up to $100 for each day that they're in violation.

In my case, however, I am the landlord, and yet the locks to my residence were illegally changed. I believe that this action should have severe repercussions because a senior citizen was illegally locked out and severely tortured with deliberation.

As you can see, my rights were outright denied, and that too with confidence. Moreover, it is a pity that the law enforcement agencies did not help me despite being spectators to these adverse conditions. However, I believe that educating people about these frequently occurring crimes can pronounce a difference. So, my dear readers, please be the ripple to my story and help many others like me retrieve our personal possessions, and most importantly, mental health and peace.

Chapter 6: Law?

I had been fortunate to be surrounded by supporting people in my devastating times. I felt defeated, but these people lifted my spirit and helped me fight through the dark. I am gratified to call these people my friends and my support system.

Firstly, I would like to acknowledge my brother Stanley's support at this time. He is my twin brother who looks exactly like me but has a story of woe written differently.

He fought in the military and, as a result, acquired the savior's pride - a wound on his leg. Of course, that injury marked the end of his career as a warrior, but I must say that his spirit and zeal still ignites ever so brightly. I can find deep wisdom embedded in his eyes, and the wrinkles on his face tell a tale that one can't unsee. Oh, that sure helps with his introverted nature.

He speaks calculative, but even his words, no matter if gibberish, have always soothed me in my difficult times. I love his company, and I am glad to be his companion.

Speaking of companionship, we, unfortunately, share the experience of being plundered as senior citizens. You already know my story, so let's talk about Stanley's experience. However, before I begin, please note that at some places, our anguish was mutual.

Stanley was adopted by Aunt Helen (Ms. Davis), so he was the rightful heir of her property after her demise. But that did not last long, thanks to Michael Abounassar, who also happened to cremate my 100-year-old aunt, Lucy Jones.

Abounassar was my distant friend, with whom I had lost touch. I met him after many years, and...I wish that I could turn back the clock and never see him again.

Gradually, he became closer to my family, and taking advantage of Stanley's soft demeanor, he tried to take everything away from Stanley. In doing so, he conspired with David Gill and filed bankruptcy for my brother and me.

They had no right to do that, but they hired an attorney, whose surname I recall was Murray. Here, I would like to mention Timonthy J Yoo, who conspired with Abounassar and Gill, handing them our property papers, despite being the court trustee.

With our property papers stolen, I believe it was the government's duty to support us in such a rough time. But, no, we had further adversity written in our fate.

In those days, Mr. Nickson was a nortary public who was, ironically, employed to deter fraud and help people, like

Stanley and me, receive justice. However, his actions ensured the contrary.

I don't know how Abounassar and Gill convinced Nickson, but they were able to make Nickson do what they wanted. Long story short, Nickson forged my late aunt Helen's signature on their drafted papers, making our claims futile.

They did not stop there; Gill sold the house property in Los Angeles and took $13,000 profit…profit from making two senior citizens miserable. Abounassar, on the other hand, used the quitclaim deed to his benefit; he made sure that we were deprived of other properties too. In fact, his whole family wronged Stanley and me in one way or another.

The other beneficiaries of Abounassar's actions were Chandell Russell and Glenda (Louisiana Jones). I blame all of them for making us suffer. These people knowingly made us vulnerable, and I believe that the right thing to do is punish them lawfully.

Other than these legal matters, there were other people who sought their share in looting us. One of them was Sydney Winfield, who stole keys to Stanley's house. Undoubtedly, he was a fine handyman as he succeeded in taking our credit cards and spent the money well by buying his brother a refrigerator.

Another character that harmed my family and me financially was Diane Jones. We had hired her as a housekeeper for my house, and her primary job was to look after my then-alive wife. Well, she just bagged all the money from my house and from our reserves in the bank. Interestingly, when I wrote to the bank about the discrepancy in my account, they denied my claim without initiating any investigation.

I have attached evidence to everything I have mentioned in this book at the end. I have nothing left to say but to urge people to help develop a legal system that can punish crooks on a larger scale. Otherwise, these crooks will goge our flesh like vultures without even realizing it.

Nowadays, Stanley and I are living together since we have no one but each other. Together, we still believe that you, my readers, could help us retrieve justice. We have not lost faith in the goodness of the world, and we are sure that one day help will arrive.

Chapter 7: Santa Monica

Some places act like our eternal calling. I say this a lot, and if this statement appears incomprehensible to you, let me explain and then proceed to the beginning of a new chapter in my life.

It was the year 1985, and I was looking for a job. I didn't have any job specifications, and I was okay with the one that fulfilled my everyday needs. So, I was applying, and I was also receiving responses, but the things did not pan out between these respondents and me because of one reason or another—I believe it was a Divine doing.

Well, one day, I received a positive answer to my application from Santa Monica Police Station. Everything went smoothly, and I was hired as the custodian. It was a good day, given I was able to support my wife and young children.

But, of course, the questions about the environment, people, and work pressure lingered in my mind.

What if I am not good enough?

What if the environment is intoxicating? I mean, there are criminals there. Is it safe for me to work there?

The people there…well, they deal with thugs on a daily basis. What will they be like? Will I fit in?

These thoughts infiltrated my mind and stopped me from taking the leap. I evaluated each aspect, put together two and two, and still chickened out. I was not sure…but deep down, I believed I belonged there.

One day, as I was talking to my wife, I realized that she believed in me to the extent I could never imagine. I still recall our conversation from that day, the one that made the decision for me.

"Honey, what are you doing?" my wife said, tapping my shoulder and sitting next to me.

"Umm…nothing, just the job stuff."

"Oh, what about the place that shortlisted you last week?"

"The police station one?"

"Yeah! I think it suits you. The way you look after our family and me, I believe you will be a great asset to Santa Monica!"

"Really?" I said and tried to read my wife's eyes, wondering if she was teasing me.

"Yes, really," she responded innocently, looking back into my eyes.

And that was the moment where I realized that I could not escape situations just because they appeared challenging to me. My wife had high expectations from me, and it was my duty to live up to those. So, I decided to consider the position at Santa Monica.

I have received many awards during and after my two decade long service at the police station.

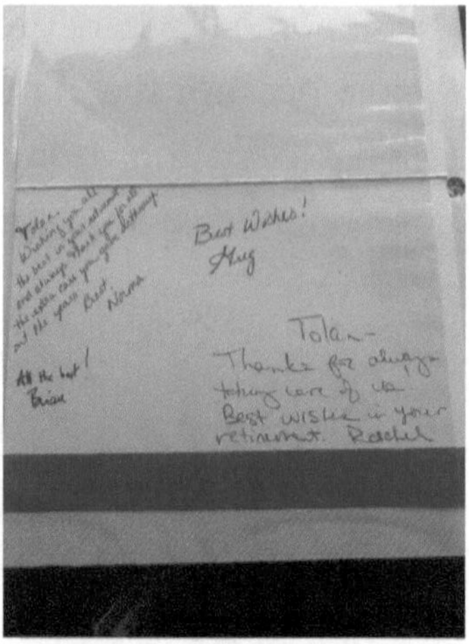

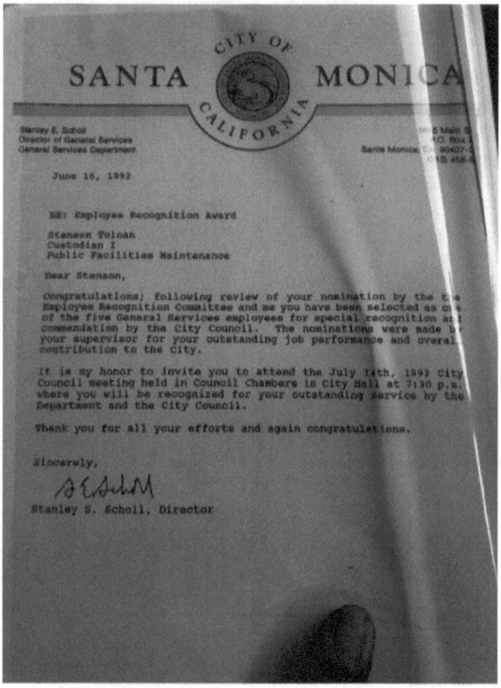

SANTA CITY OF CALIFORNIA MONICA

Stanley E. Scholl
Director of General Services
General Services Department

Santa Monica, CA 90407-

June 16, 1992

RE: Employee Recognition Award

Stenson Toloan
Custodian I
Public Facilities Maintenance

Dear Stenson,

Congratulations; following review of your nomination by the the Employee Recognition Committee and me you have been selected as one of the five General Services employees for special recognition and commendation by the City Council. The nominations were made by your supervisor for your outstanding job performance and overall contribution to the City.

It is my honor to invite you to attend the July 14th, 1992 City Council meeting held in Council Chambers in City Hall at 7:30 p.m. where you will be recognized for your outstanding service by the Department and the City Council.

Thank you for all your efforts and again congratulations.

Sincerely,

Stanley S. Scholl, Director

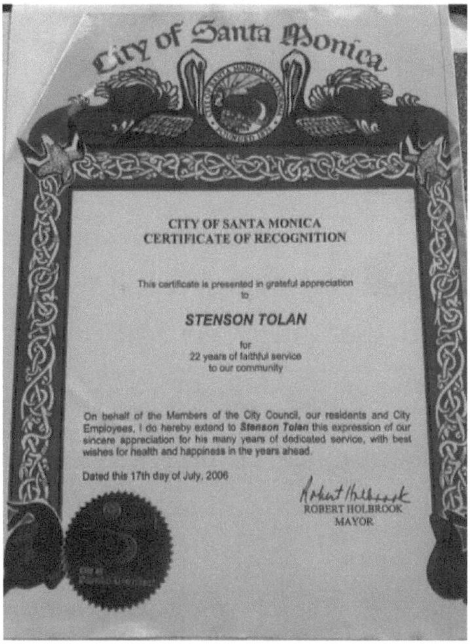

City of Santa Monica

CITY OF SANTA MONICA
CERTIFICATE OF RECOGNITION

This certificate is presented in grateful appreciation to

STENSON TOLAN

for
22 years of faithful service
to our community

On behalf of the Members of the City Council, our residents and City Employees, I do hereby extend to **Stenson Tolan** this expression of our sincere appreciation for his many years of dedicated service, with best wishes for health and happiness in the years ahead.

Dated this 17th day of July, 2006

ROBERT HOLBROOK
MAYOR

However, my favorite memory is a letter from a citizen appreciating me for returning his wallet.

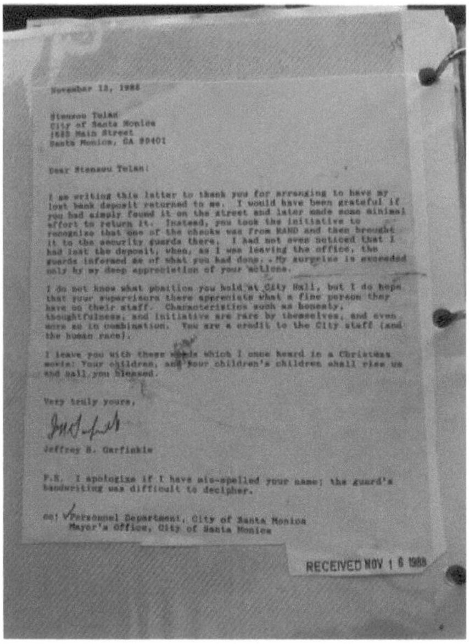

November 12, 1988

Stenson Tolan
City of Santa Monica
1685 Main Street
Santa Monica, CA 90401

Dear Stenson Tolan:

I am writing this letter to thank you for arranging to have my lost bank deposit returned to me. I would have been grateful if you had simply found it on the street and later made some minimal effort to return it. Instead, you took the initiative to recognize that one of the checks was from RAND and then brought it to the security guards there. I had not even noticed that I had lost the deposit, when, as I was leaving the office, the guards informed me of what you had done. My surprise is exceeded only by my deep appreciation of your actions.

I do not know what position you hold at City Hall, but I do hope that your supervisors there appreciate what a fine person they have on their staff. Characteristics such as honesty, thoughtfulness, and initiative are rare by themselves, and even more so in combination. You are a credit to the City staff (and the human race).

I leave you with these words which I once heard in a Christmas movie: Your children, and your children's children shall rise up and call you blessed.

Very truly yours,

Jeffrey B. Garfinkle

P.S. I apologize if I have mis-spelled your name; the guard's handwriting was difficult to decipher.

cc: Personnel Department, City of Santa Monica
Mayor's Office, City of Santa Monica

RECEIVED NOV 16 1988

Having said that, I also met people during this time who made me believe that good and evil coexist. The people who were on the negative end of the spectrum were Ralph Harrison and Joyce, my supervisor.

I was helping Harrison with some matters, but he was not only arrogant but disrespectful toward me. In contrast, Joyce captured the entire incident on her personal phone, which is not only an invasion of privacy but also an illegal act.

Still, in a nutshell, the experience at Santa Monica was great and had taught me valuable life lessons.

Chapter 8: A Ray of Hope

It is not easy to expose the ones you love, but it is also not easy to see your lifelong savings go to waste in a matter of time.

I never thought I would have to confront my son and his girlfriend publicly, through a book…through my heartfelt words, and through my heartache.

But this is necessary. This is important to put an end to such a vice penetrating its claws in our society. It is pertinent to expose such people so that senior citizens like me can safeguard themselves better.

I have highlighted in this book almost everything one needs to know to protect themselves. From my personal experience to all the involved laws, so that you can use this information and do the needful to avoid ending where I am today.

Also, I will advise people to steer clear of the people I have mentioned in the book. They would do nothing to help you and would just waste your time and energy. Having said that, I really hope that our system improves and puts an end to the miseries of many like us. It is actually this vile system that facilitates people like my son and his girlfriend to get away with anything and everything.

As for me, I'm not hopeless, for I know I will get justice one day. I believe people like you can amplify my voice and help me retrieve my belongings.

Optimism is a part of my belief now; I will keep fighting until the end, and I urge you to do the same.

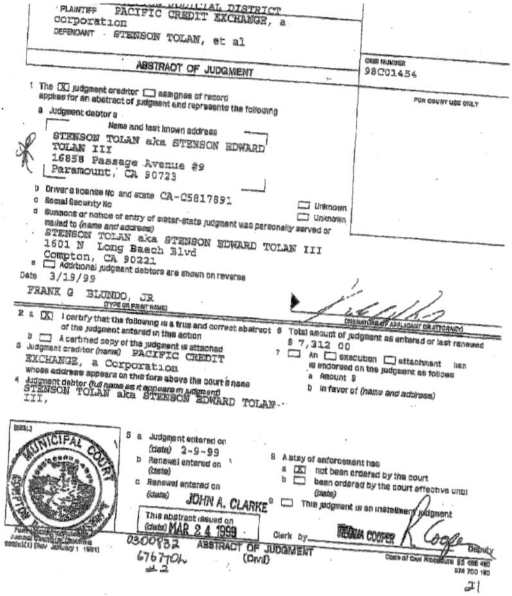

PLAINTIFF PACIFIC CREDIT EXCHANGE, a corporation

DEFENDANT STENSON TOLAN, et al

ABSTRACT OF JUDGMENT

CASE NUMBER 98C01454

FOR COURT USE ONLY

1 The [X] judgment creditor [ ] assignee of record applies for an abstract of judgment and represents the following

a Judgment debtor's

Name and last known address

STENSON TOLAN aka STENSON EDWARD TOLAN III
16858 Passage Avenue #9
Paramount, CA 90723

b Driver's license No and state CA-C5817891 [ ] Unknown

c Social Security No [ ] Unknown

d Summons or notice of entry of sister-state judgment was personally served or mailed to (name and address)

STENSON TOLAN aka STENSON EDWARD TOLAN III
1601 N Long Beach Blvd
Compton, CA 90221

e [ ] Additional judgment debtors are shown on reverse

Date 3/19/99

FRANK G BLUNDO, JR
(TYPE OR PRINT NAME)

(SIGNATURE OF APPLICANT OR ATTORNEY)

2 a [X] I certify that the following is a true and correct abstract of the judgment entered in this action

b [ ] A certified copy of the judgment is attached

3 Judgment creditor (name) PACIFIC CREDIT EXCHANGE, a Corporation whose address appears on this form above the court's name

4 Judgment debtor (full name as it appears in judgment) STENSON TOLAN aka STENSON EDWARD TOLAN III,

6 Total amount of judgment as entered or last renewed $ 7,312 00

7 [ ] An [ ] execution [ ] attachment lien is endorsed on the judgment as follows

a Amount $

b In favor of (name and address)

(SEAL)

MUNICIPAL COURT COMPTON

5 a Judgment entered on (date) 2-9-99

b Renewal entered on (date)

c Renewal entered on (date)

JOHN A. CLARKE

This abstract issued on (date) MAR 2 4 1999

8 A stay of enforcement has

a [X] not been ordered by the court

b [ ] been ordered by the court effective until (date)

9 [ ] This judgment is an installment judgment

Clerk by REGINA COOPER, Deputy

ABSTRACT OF JUDGMENT (Civil)

Judicial Council of California 982(a)(1) [Rev January 1 1991]

Code of Civil Procedure §§ 488 480, 674 700 190

0300832
6767704
#2

21

Pre-Court Filing Report
April 26, 2012
Stenson Edward Tolan Jr.II (Father) v. Stenson Edward Tolan III (Son) et al.
Elder Financial Abuse

April 22, 1999	$7,312 Lien Placed on Client's Home for Son's Debt
Unknown Date	Son and Girlfriend Move into Client's Home
January 26, 2005	Son Tricks Client into Signing Over Home
Unknown Date	Son and Girlfriend Illegally Evict Client
July 23, 2007	Son Takes Out $60,000 Loan on Home
December 11, 2010	Client's Wife, Lois Tolan, Dies
Exact Date Unknown - 2011	Client Discovers Fraudulent Deed Transfer

April 22, 1999 - $7, 312 Lien Placed on Client's Home for Son's Debt

Attorney Frank Blundo SBN 79793 filed an abstract of judgment on April 22, 2012 against the home with the registrar recorder's office for $7,312. The creditor is listed as "Pacific Credit Exchange, a corporation." The judgment debtor is listed as "Stenson Tolan aka Stenson Edward Tolan III." The drivers license number, social security number, and address of the debtor are all those of the Son, not the Client.

Unknown Date – Son and Girlfriend Move into Client's Home

Son told Client that he needed a place to stay and pled with Client to help him but refused to say what, if anything, was wrong.

At the time Son lived with his Girlfriend, Tabby Mason, possibly in Paramount, and worked for Golden State Dental in Compton making dental molds. It is believed he is still employed there. The full legal name of Girlfriend is not known.

Client agreed to let Son move but did not discuss any details of the arrangement with Son. A short time later, Son moved in with Girlfriend. Client was surprised because there had never been any discussion about Girlfriend moving in.

Immediately Client felt uncomfortable in his own home. Client was scared of Son's temper and did not confront him about Girlfriend moving in. Girlfriend made comments to the effect that they moved in to help him and save the house and they were doing Client a favor. When Girlfriend would say these things, Son would just be quiet.

Client was experiencing severe migraine headaches at the time. Much of it was due to his high blood pressure and the stresses related to his wife being in a nursing home, being his brother's caregiver, and his involvement in a complicated on-going lawsuit that eventually went to trial in which, ironically, his Brother, Stenley Tolan, was a victim of fraud related to elder abuse and real estate. After Son and Girlfriend moved in, Client started to feel more and more sick when at his house and especially when around Son and Girlfriend. Client got more headaches and they

became more severe. He never ate any meals with Son and Girlfriend and they never offered to cook or have any meals with him. Girlfriend was cold and not friendly towards him.

January 26, 2005 – Son Tricks Client into Signing Over Home

Client signed grant deed giving house to Son. The document states "This is a Bonafide Gift and the Grantors Received Nothing in Return." This occurred in the office of Notary Jaime Saavedra (COMM #1431935). Client signed his name and his wife's name to the deed. Client held the property in joint tenancy with his wife. His wife was still alive at the time.

On the day the document was signed, Son called Client from work and told him to meet him at the office of the notary. Son said he needed Client's help right away and that it was urgent. Son would not give details, but instead gave an address in Compton for Client to immediately go. Client tried asking Son what was so important and whether it was something that could be handled at a later time. Son insisted that, whatever it was, it could not.

Client drove with his brother to the Notary. When he got there, his head was beating and he was not feeling good in any way. He had a severe migraine. He signed the document but did not know that he was giving away his home right then and there. He thought he was just signing a document that would leave the house to his son when he died. He never signed any notary book and was not fingerprinted. The notary, who appeared to be in his 50s or 60s, several times told Client, "Don't Tell Anybody. You Were Here," and shook his finger at him as he said this. Client said to his Son that there was "something fishy about this notary." The son just responded that it was "going to be alright" and that "nothing was wrong." Client expressed several more reservations. Then Son got silent like he was mad. Then Son said, "I don't want to deal with you no more!" and left the room. As this was all occurring, Client's headache got worse and worse. It was very intense and his head eventually was pounding. Client signed the document. Outside the notary's office he said to his son, "I didn't give you the house you know." Son was just silent."

Client thought that the document he was signing just meant that when he died, or if anything ever happened to him like he needed to be in a nursing home, the house would go to his son. He had never signed any type of trust, will, or death/incapacity planning documents before.

Client's Brother sat in car in parking lot of notary's office when all this occurred since he has difficulty walking on his own. Son parked on another side of the building so Brother never saw Son enter or leave the building. As soon as Client got back in car and told Brother what

Tolan Pre Court Filing Report
April 26, 2012
Page 3 of 5

happened, Brother expressed numerous expressions of distrust regarding the Son and what had transpired.

Client believes that Notary was recommended by Girlfriend's Mother, Patricia Mason who also works at Golden Dental. This is only a hunch the Client has without any direct or corroborating evidence.

In the years previous to the signing Client had discussed with his wife leaving the house after they died to Son and only other child, a daughter, from whom he is also estranged. He and his wife were not even ecstatic about doing this due to their children's ongoing bad behavior. After they discussed it though they felt that "blood was blood" and would leave the house to their children. Neither Client nor his wife ever intended to give either of the children the house in any way while they were still alive.

Unknown Date – Son and Girlfriend Illegally Evict Client

At the time, as previously mentioned, Client was serving as Brother's caregiver. Brother lives about two miles away from Client's home. Client was regularly going back and forth between the two residences. While he had some items at Brother's house, all of Client's clothes and possessions were at his home. Client went to his home on a daily basis to check on his possessions, get his mail and a change of clothes, and get any items he needed to take care of his Brother and Brother's house.

One day Client went to the front door of his home and the key would not turn. He knew right away that the locks had been changed. Client knew this because he had installed the locks himself. His blood pressure immediately went up as he realized what Son had done.

Client knocked on the door and rang the doorbell. Both Son and Girlfriend each separately turned back the curtain on the front window, looked right at him, and went back inside. They did not answer the door or say anything. He could not go to the back or side of his home because there were fences and gates preventing entry to the sides and back of the house. Client himself had installed these.

Client walked back to his car and got in. Brother was in the car. Client told Brother what happened. They discussed it and both were very upset. In the days and months that followed, Client contacted various law enforcement agencies, government offices, and low-income legal services, but did not receive any assistance.

Tolan Pre Court Filing Report
April 26, 2012
Page 4 of 5

Client called home a lot at first to confront Son and Girlfriend. The Son was often just silent and said nothing. Client thinks Son may have recorded him. One time the Son said "I'll get an attorney and fight you the whole way." Client eventually stopped calling them.

Note: It is unclear exactly when the following event occurred. Client recounted it several times but gave different time periods for each recounting.

Client used to drive by home a lot to look at it. One day when he drove by, he saw large commercial size dumpsters parked in front of it. It looked like the kitchen was being remodeled. He also saw many of his possessions and memories in the dumpster or thrown on the ground around the dumpster. This included, among many other things, all his tools from the garage, a special chair he had purchased for his wife, and his couch. Then he saw Son, Girlfriend, and Girlfriends Mother come out of the house. He approached them. They were surprised to see him.

Client asked what they were doing and why all his possessions were in the dumpsters or out on the street. They said they were going to put everything back but to Client it was obvious they were throwing everything out. He asked them repeatedly when he was going to get his house back. His son at first would not answer. Then his son started saying that he couldn't "give it back right now." Then Son told him that he was not going to get "a G** D*** thing" and then said several times "I don't want to talk to you. I don't want to talk to you." The Son smelled strongly of marijuana. When confronted about the loan against the house, Son replied that he and Girlfriend were going to pay it back.

After this, Client stopped driving by the home because it hurt him too much.

July 23, 2007 – Son Takes Out $60,000 Loan on Home

Bank of America recorded a short form deed of trust against the property and is listed on the document as the trustee/beneficiary. The title company listed on the recording was United General Title Insurance of Rocky Hill, CT. The loan number is 68249018392599. The trustor is listed as PRLAP, Inc. The name on the document is "Stenson E. Tolan." It is signed by a "Stenson E. Tolan" but the signature does not look similar to the other documents with the signature of Client. The name of the Notary who notarized the signature was Notary Adriana L. Ramos (Commission #1617681).

December 11, 2010 – Client's Wife Dies

Client's Wife Lois died in the Sun Ray Nursing Home in Los Angeles. The death certificate lists the causes of death as cardiopulmonary arrest, organic heart disease, and arteriosclerosis heart

Tolan Pre Court Filing Report
April 26, 2012
Page 5 of 5

disease. The home will not release any of her records without a court order. Client estimates that wife was in home for between five to seven years.

Exact Date Unknown – Sometime in 2011 – Client Discovers Fraudulent Deed Transfer and Liens on Property

After wife dies, Client learns of the loans taken out against the house and that the deed filed at the recorder's office indicate that he does not own his home.

Washington Mutual

January 4, 2000

Stanley Tolan
1051 W. 64th St. Apt. 2
Los Angeles, CA 90044

Dear Mr. Tolan:

Mr. Killinger has received your letter and requested that I respond on his behalf. Thank you for taking the time to write. We are very interested in addressing your concerns.

It is our understanding that you believe Ms. Diane Adams "deceived" your elderly aunt, Ms. Lucy Jones, by taking her down to the bank and adding her name to your aunt's account. You are requesting an investigation into this matter.

Please accept our apologies for any frustration this matter may have caused. We appreciate your concerns, and recognize the importance of providing superior service. To honor your request we conducted an investigation and the results do not indicate any error on the part of the Bank. Also, the results do not indicate any intent by Ms. Adams to deceive Ms. Jones. However, if Ms. Jones desires to change the vesting of the account in question, she may do so in writing.

Thank you for allowing us the opportunity to address your concerns.

Sincerely,

Sebastian Bologna
Quality Service Management

cc: Kerry Killinger, Chairman, President and Chief Executive Officer

9200 Oakdale Ave.
Chatsworth, CA 91311

the LEONE LAW GROUP
Criminal Defense - Victims Rights
Restraining Orders - Police Misconduct
Alcohol/Police Permit Regulations

10100 Santa Monica Blvd.
Third Floor
Century City, California 90067
Phone: (310) 651-9912
Fax: (310) 772-2246

April 26, 2012

Stenson E. Tolan Jr.
2115 West 28th St.
Los Angeles, CA 90018

Dear Mr. Tolan:

**Re: PRE-COURT FILING REPORT
CLIENT STATEMENT AND
SUGGESTED ACTION LIST**

I have completed a thorough investigation into all of the facts surrounding your son and his girlfriend taking your home away from you, illegally evicting you from it, and using the equity in it to benefit financially. Attached is a copy of the report.

There are still many questions. They cannot be answered though until some sort of court action is initiated, Then we would have the authority to compel individuals and entities to turn over certain documents to us and/or formally answer questions. The bottom line though is that you have a strong, but not necessarily quick or easy, case against your son and his girlfriend. You also have a case against Bank of America and the various other individuals and entities involved in placing the two different liens on your home. We do not know enough at this point to say how strong a case though we have against them.

The attached Client Statement is for $1,111.01. This brings the total you will have paid for my time and expenses to $3,111.01. This is the estimate I originally gave you for a full pre-court filing investigation. As we previously discussed, a proper and thorough pre-court filing investigation can save a lot in time and money when and if any court action is initiated.

Page Two of Two
April 26, 2012
Letter to Stenson E. Tolan Jr.

When I have received the final full payment due I will meet with you and your sister Evelyn to explain in detail the costs, risks, and challenges that are involved should you decide you want to initiate a court action. If we go forth with a court case I want you to be fully informed regarding these issues.

I have also enclosed a list of recommended actions you take in the meantime. These are actions that I believe will be helpful to you regardless of how you decide to proceed.

Respectfully,

Damian Leone
Attorney at Law

DL/dl

Enclosures (3)

2

09/06/07

20072073508

Recording Requested By
Bank of America, NA

Record and Return To:
United General Title Ins
Fiserv--27 Inwood Road
ROCKY HILL, CT 06067
Loan Number: 68249018392599

Tolan, Stenson E

[Space Above This Line For Recording Data]

SHORT FORM DEED OF TRUST
(EQUITY MAXIMIZER ACCOUNT)

This Deed of Trust is made on JULY 23, 2007 by STENSON E TOLAN

(collectively and individually "Trustor") PRLAP, INC ("Trustee"), and the beneficiary, Bank of America, N.A ("Bank") Trustee is a subsidiary of Bank Any non-titleholder signs below as Trustor solely for the purpose of subjecting any community property interest in the property described below to this Deed of Trust The words "I," "me," and "my" in this Deed of Trust refer to the Trustor, whether one or more

BANK AND I AGREE:

1. **Property Security.** For the purpose of securing the obligations described below, I irrevocably grant, convey, transfer and assign to Trustee, in trust with power of sale, the property located in LOS ANGELES County, California described as follows
SCHEDULE A ATTACHED HERETO AND MADE A PART OF.

with the street address 1539 W 94TH ST, LOS ANGELES, CALIFORNIA 90047-3913 and with Parcel No 6055-001-017 and including all improvements and fixtures now or later erected on the property, and all easements, rights, appurtenances and fixtures now or later a part of or related to the above described property (collectively the "Property").

2. **This Deed of Trust secures:**
   - All of the obligations of the borrowers under the Disclosure and Loan Agreement dated JULY 23, 2007 , and naming STENSON E TOLAN

STENSON E TOLAN/99507199162110 0
CALIFORNIA SHORT FORM DEED OF TRUST
(EQUITY MAXIMIZER ACCOUNT)
CAHESISF BOA 02/02/07

Page 1 of 3

DocMagic eForms 800-649-1362
www.docmagic.com

4

[Space Below This Line For Acknowledgment]

State of California)
) ss
County of LOS ANGELES)

On July 23, 2007 before me, Adriana I Ramos Notary Public

personally appeared STENSON E TOLAN

~~personally known to me~~ (or proved to me on the basis of satisfactory evidence) to be the person(s) whose name(s) is/are subscribed to the within instrument and acknowledged to me that he/she/they executed the same in his/her/their authorized capacity(ies), and that by his/her/their signature(s) on the instrument the person(s), or the entity upon behalf of which the person(s) acted, executed the instrument

WITNESS my hand and official seal

ADRIANA I. RAMOS
Commission # 1617681
Notary Public - California
Los Angeles County
My Comm. Expires Nov 1, 2009

NOTARY SEAL

Adriana I Ramos
NOTARY SIGNATURE

Adriana I Ramos
(Typed Name of Notary)

STENSON E TOLAN/995071991621100
CALIFORNIA SHORT FORM DEED OF TRUST
(EQUITY MAXIMIZER ACCOUNT)
CAHESISF BOA 02/02/07

Page 3 of 3

DocMagic eForms 800-649-1362
www.docmagic.com

Name / Street Address / City & State

STENSON E. TOLAN, JR.
1539 West 94th Street
Los Angeles, Calif. 90047

RECORDED IN OFFICIAL RECORDS
OF LOS ANGELES COUNTY, CA
27 MIN. PAST 11 A.M. MAY 4 1978
Recorder's Office

SPACE ABOVE THIS LINE FOR RECORDER'S USE

FEE $3 G

DECLARATION OF HOMESTEAD

(JOINT DECLARATION OF HUSBAND AND WIFE)

STENSON E. TOLAN, JR. (Name of Husband) and LOIS TOLAN (Name of Wife)

do severally certify and declare as follows:

(1) They are husband and wife.

(2) STENSON E. TOLAN, JR. (Name of Husband) is the head of a family, consisting of himself and wife, LOIS TOLAN, and their minor children, Stenson E. Tolan, III, age 8, and LISA TOLAN, age 4

(3) They are now residing on the land and premises located in the City of LOS ANGELES

County of LOS ANGELES State of California, and more particularly described as follows:

Lot 549 of Tract No. 6084 as per map recorded in Book 101, Page 53-57 of Maps, in the office of the County Recorder of said County,

and commonly known as 1539 West 94th Street, Los Angeles, Calif. 90047.

(4) They claim the land and premises hereinabove described together with the dwelling house thereon, and its appurtenances, as a Homestead.

(5) No former declaration of homestead has been made by them, or by either of them, except as follows:[1] None.

(6) The character of said property so sought to be homesteaded, and the improvements thereon may generally be described as follows:[2]
Three bedroom single family dwelling and detached single garage.

IN WITNESS WHEREOF, they have hereunto set their hands this 1st day of May 19 78.

x Stenson E. Tolan Jr
Stenson E. Tolan Jr. (Husband)

Lois Tolan
Lois Tolan (Wife)

Footnotes 1 and 2: See Reverse Side.

STATE OF CALIFORNIA
COUNTY OF LOS ANGELES } ss.

On May 1st 19 78 before me, the undersigned, a Notary Public in and for said State, personally appeared STENSON E. TOLAN, JR. and LOIS TOLAN known to me to be the persons whose names are subscribed to the within instrument, and severally acknowledged to me that they executed the same.

Witness my hand and official seal.

Elva Jean Drake
Notary Public in and for said State.

OFFICIAL SEAL
ELVA JEAN DRAKE
NOTARY PUBLIC - CALIFORNIA
LOS ANGELES COUNTY
My comm. expires MAY 15, 1981
1331 Los Florence Ave., Los Angeles, CA 90001

STATE OF CALIFORNIA
COUNTY OF LOS ANGELES } ss.

STENSON E. TOLAN, JR. and LOIS TOLAN husband and wife, each being first duly sworn, deposes and says: That he/she is one of the declarants in the foregoing declaration of homestead; that he/she has read the foregoing declaration and knows the contents thereof, and that the matters therein stated are true of his/her own knowledge.

x Stenson E. Tolan Jr (Husband)

Lois Tolan (Wife)

Subscribed and Sworn to before me on May 1st, 19 78

Elva Jean Drake
Notary Public in and for said State.

OFFICIAL SEAL
ELVA JEAN DRAKE
NOTARY PUBLIC - CALIFORNIA
LOS ANGELES COUNTY
My comm. expires MAY 15, 1981
1331 Los Florence Ave., Los Angeles, CA 90001

WOLCOTTS FORM 784—HOMESTEAD—JOINT DECLARATION OF HUSBAND AND WIFE—Rev. 2-73

CALIFORNIA ALL-PURPOSE ACKNOWLEDGEMENT 05 0049878

4

State of California

County of Los Angeles

On January 6 2005 before me, Jaime Saavedra (Name and Title of Officer (e.g., "Jane Doe, Notary Public"))

personally appeared Stenson E Tolan JR & Lois Tolan (Name(s) of Signer(s))

☐ personally known to me -OR- ☐ proved to me on the basis of satisfactory evidence to be the person(s) whose name(s) is/are subscribed to the within instrument and acknowledged to me that he/she/they executed the same in his/her/their authorized capacity(ies), and that by his/her/their signature(s) on the instrument the person(s), or the entity upon behalf of which the person(s) acted, executed the instrument.

JAIME SAAVEDRA
COMM. #1431935
Notary Public-California
LOS ANGELES COUNTY
My Comm. Exp. Aug 19, 2007

WITNESS my hand and official seal

Signature of Notary Public

OPTIONAL

Though the information below is not required by law, it may prove valuable to persons relying on the document and could prevent fraudulent removal and reattachment of this form to another document

Description of Attached Document

Title or Type of Document Grant Deed

Number of Pages

Document Date

Signer(s) Other Than Named Above

Capacity(ies) Claimed by Signer(s)

Signer's Name

☐ Individual
☐ Corporate Officer
☐ Titles(s):
☐ Partner - ☐ Limited ☐ General
☐ Attorney-in-Fact
☐ Trustee
☐ Guardian or Conservator
☐ Other:

Signer Is Representing

RIGHT THUMBPRINT OF SIGNER
Top of Thumb here

Signer's Name

☐ Individual
☐ Corporate Officer
☐ Title(s):
☐ Partner - ☐ Limited ☐ General
☐ Attorney-in-Fact
☐ Trustee
☐ Guardian or Conservator
☐ Other

Signer Is Representing

RIGHT THUMBPRINT OF SIGNER
Top of Thumb here

STEALING BAD BUSINESS

WHERE IS THE OWNERS FINGER PRINT STENSON E TOLAN JR WHERE IS THE DRIVER LICENSE FRAUD

LOS ANGELES,CA
Document: D 2005.49878

Page 4 of 4

Printed on 12/10/2013 10:35:45 AM

and Tax Statement To:

Helen Mae Davis
2115 W. 28th Street
Los Angeles, CA 90018

Escrow No.
Title Order No.
APN:

SPACE ABOVE THIS LINE FOR RECORDER'S USE

QUITCLAIM DEED

The undersigned grantor(s) declare(s)
Documentary transfer tax is $ -0- City tax $
[ ] computed on full value of property conveyed, or
[ ] computed on full value less value of liens or encumbrances remaining at time of sale,
[ ] Unincorporated Area City of

FOR A VALUABLE CONSIDERATION, receipt of which is hereby acknowledged,

HELEN M. DAVIS, a single woman as her sole separate property

hereby remises, releases and quitclaims to HELEN MAE DAVIS, Trustee ofthe Helen Mae Davis 1997 Revocable Living Trust, executed on July 8, 1997, all her rights, title and interest in

the following described real property in the City of Los Angeles
County of Los Angeles State of Calif

Lot 10 of the West Adams and Western Avenue Tract, in the City of Los Angeles, State of California, as per map recorded in Book 6 Page of Maps, in the Office of the County Recorder of said county.

Commonly known as 2115 W. 28th Street, Los Angeles, CA 90018.

This conveyance transfers the grantor's interest into her revocable trust and is exempt from transfer tax under R&T Code §11911.

DATED: 7-12-02

STATE OF CALIFORNIA
COUNTY OF Los Angeles
ON July 12, 2002 before me,
HELEN M. DAVIS personally appeared

personally known to me (or proved to me on the basis of satisfactory evidence) to be the person(s) whose name(s) is/are subscribed to the within instrument and acknowledged to me that he/she/they executed the same in his/her/their authorized capacity(ies), and that by his/her/their signature(s) on the instrument the person(s), or the entity upon behalf of which the person(s) acted, executed the instrument.

Witness my hand and official seal.

Signature Sandra Nixon, Notary Public

HELEN M. Davis
Helen M. Davis
Signed by Edward M. Abounass For Helen M. Davis

SANDRA NIXON
Commission # 1281464
Notary Public — California
Los Angeles County
My Comm. Expires May 19, 2004

MAIL TAX STATEMENT AS DIRECTED ABOVE

ATD-13F (Rev 4/94) QUITCLAIM DEED

DEAR JEFF:

HERE IS THE SUPERIOR COURT CASE FILED JAN 07, 2008. TO DATE, STANLEY HAS RECEIVED BACK THE 28TH ST. HOUSE.

HE HAS NOT RECEIVED:

1. THE 55TH ST. HOUSE
2. THE OIL/GAS ROYALTIES ON 28TH ST PROPERTY.
3. THE TWO VACANT LOTS (AS DESCRIBED IN COURT DOCS).
4. THE $2,278,201.00 CASH JUDGMENT.
5. TWO CARS: '87 CHEVY CELEBRITY & '88 HONDA.
6. PUNITIVE DAMAGES OF $90,000 & $15,000 FROM HUSBAND & WIFE.

STANLEY TOLAN NEVER SIGNED ANY OF THE CRITICAL DOCUMENTS (AS WAS DETERMINED BY THE COURT).

DEFENDANT USED SIGNED PAPERWORK FROM A 2001 BANKRUPEY FILING TO PARTIALLY CLOUD THE SUPERIOR COURT'S 2007 ACTIONS IN THE CASE. TRUSTEE, DAVID GILL (LATER SHUT DOWN BY THE IRS!) PASSED TITLE TO THE 55TH ST HOUSE TO ONE OF HIS CROONIES.

TOLAN WILL PHONE YOU TO CONFIRM RECEIPT OF THESE DOCUMENTS.

Items faxed to 323-460-5333, Attention, JEFF:

1. This Cover Letter. 2. Exhibit A: 8-item signed document (summary of actions). 3. Notice of Entry of Judgment or Order, dated Aug 14, 2007 (Jon D. Ceretto, Clerk of the U.S. Bankruptcy Court, Case #2:01-12245-TD). 4. L.A. Superior Court Case #06U07343 (an 11-page document). 5. Five miscellaneous pages (6/10/09 Bankruptcy front sheet; Tax bill on 28th St.; Bankruptcy Case #BC346430, front sheet only; PXP royalty payment on 28th St property; Edward Abounassar home address information).

Thank you, Jeff;

Tolan–

RECORDING REQUESTED BY:

AND WHEN RECORDED MAIL TO:

Mr. and Mrs. Tony Vargas
440 WEST 55th STREET
LOS ANGELES, CA 90037

DAVID GILL
SALE TO
SYLVIA NAVA
V
VARGAS

03/04/2010
"20100291240"

Stenson E. Tolan Jr./II

Client Statement
the Leone Law Group

April 1, 2012 – April 30, 2012

Date	Attorney Service(s) Provided	Time Devoted
April 5 2012	Client Interview	25 minutes
April 10 2012	Reviewed Property Documents Obtained from County Recorder	1 hour 30 minutes
	Follow-Up Calls for Client Medical Files	
April 18 2012	Drafted Pre-Litigation Case Report, Case Timeline, and List of Potential Witnesses and Defendants	1 hour 10 minutes
April 24 2012	Drafted/Revised Pre-Litigation Report, Case Timeline, and List of Potential Witnesses and Defendants	3 hours 15 minutes
Various Dates	Phone Calls to/from Client	Not Charged on this Statement
Subtotal Attorney Time - 6.3 hours x $200/hr		$1,260
Expense		Cost
mileage		$7.77
10% administrative fee per fee agreement		$126.00
Subtotal Expenses		$133.77
Total Due for This Statement Period		$1,393.77
Amount Due from Last Statement		$717.24
Payment Received Since Last Statement		$1,000.00
Balance – Amount Now Due		$1,111.01

Remit payment to:

Damian Leone
the Leone Law Group
10100 Santa Monica Blvd. Third Floor
Century City, CA 90067

PS2-92

SERVICE LIST

UNITED STATES TRUSTEE
725 S. FIGUEROA ST. 26TH FLOOR
LOS ANGELES, CA 90017

CHAPTER 7 TRUSTEE
DAVID A. GILL
2029 CENTURY PARK EAST, THIRD FLOOR
LOS ANGELES, CA 90067
VIA HAND DELIVERY

DEFENDANTS

DEBTOR
STANLEY TOLAN
2115 W. 28TH STREET
LOS ANGELES, CA 90018

COUNSEL FOR STANLEY TOLAN)
ALFRED ANYIA, ESQ.
LAW OFFICES OF ALFRED O. ANYIA
880 W. FIRST STREET, #108
LOS ANGELES, CA 90012

CHAPTER 7 TRUSTEE OF EDWARD AND AYEDA ABOUNASSAR
TIMOTHY J. YOO
ROBINSON, DIAMANT & WOLKOWITZ
1888 CENTURY PARK EAST, STE 1500
LOS ANGELES, CA 90067

ATTORNEYS FOR DEFENDANTS EDWARD AND AYEDA ABOUNASSAR
ARMEN SHAGHZO, ESQ.
SHAGHZO & SHAGHZO
535 N. BRAND BLVD., SUITE 502
GLENDALE, CA 91203

EDWARD AND AIDA ABOUNASSAR
731 EAST CYPRESS STREET
GLENDALE, CA 92105

WASHINGTON MUTUAL BANK, FA
LEGAL DEPARTMENT
ATTN: ALLEN FISHMAN, CEO
1301 2ND AVE.
WMC 3501
SEATTLE, WA 98101
VIA CERTIFIED MAIL

WASHINGTON MUTUAL BANK, FA
LEGAL DEPARTMENT
ATTN: MICHAEL SOLENDER (CHIEF LEGAL OFFICER)
1301 2ND AVE.
WMC 3501
SEATTLE, WA 98101
VIA CERTIFIED MAIL

Jul 26 21, 07:07p STENSON TOLAN 323-643-4208 p.17

RECORDING REQUESTED BY:

AND WHEN RECORDED MAIL TO:

Mr. and Mrs. Tony Vargas
440 WEST 55th STREET
LOS ANGELES, CA 90037

DAVID GILL
SALE TO
SYLVIA NOVA
V
VARGAS

03/04/2010
"20100291240"

Stenson E. Tolan Jr./II

Client Statement
the Leone Law Group

April 1, 2012 – April 30, 2012

Date	Attorney Service(s) Provided	Time Devoted
April 5 2012	Client Interview	25 minutes
April 10 2012	Reviewed Property Documents Obtained from County Recorder	1 hour 30 minutes
	Follow-Up Calls for Client Medical Files	
April 18 2012	Drafted Pre-Litigation Case Report, Case Timeline, and List of Potential Witnesses and Defendants	1 hour 10 minutes
April 24 2012	Drafted/Revised Pre-Litigation Report, Case Timeline, and List of Potential Witnesses and Defendants	3 hours 15 minutes
Various Dates	Phone Calls to/from Client	Not Charged on this Statement
Subtotal Attorney Time - 6.3 hours x $200/hr		$1,260
Expense		Cost
mileage		$7.77
10% administrative fee per fee agreement		$126.00
Subtotal Expenses		$133.77
Total Due for This Statement Period		$1,393.77
Amount Due from Last Statement		$717.24
Payment Received Since Last Statement		$1,000.00
Balance – Amount Now Due		$1,111.01

Remit payment to:

Damian Leone
the Leone Law Group
10100 Santa Monica Blvd. Third Floor
Century City, CA 90067

December 3' 011

To whom it may Concern:

The property at 1539 W. 94th Street in Los Angeles, Ca. 90047 is my house Stenton Tolan. I wanted to add my son name onto the house so just in case something happen to me. In the process of doing the paperwork my son removed my name from the property, at the time my wife was very ill and my brother was too. I moved out of my house into the house with my brother to take care of him for a short time until he was feeling better. I told my son to move into my house so it wouldn't be vacant while I was staying with my brother. He wouldn't have to pay rent because the house was paid off. Shorty after my son moved into the house with his girlfriend.

Then my son went and got a loan on the house without my permission. I found out, he then told me that this was his house now. He treated me into signing my name completing off the property when we was just suppose to be adding his name with my name in case of a emergency. I didn't understand what I was signing I trusted my son and he sold my property and I want it back.

Sincerely,

Stenton Tolan

Jul 26 21, 07:02p STENSON TOLAN 323-643-4208 p.2

(310) 674-5353
Internal Medicine

October 19, 2015

To: Whom it may concern

Fr: Alvin Trotter, M.D.

Re: *Stinson Tolan*

Mr. Tolan is a long-term patient of mine. Mr. Tolan told me that his son had taken his house and that he had borrowed $60,000.00 against his house. He is under a great deal of stress due to this matter between him and his son.

Mr. Tolan has reported multiple issues with his son he is stressed due to the loss of his home. He states he had no understanding that paperwork he signed would cause the loss of his home.

If you have any questions, or need additional information, please feel free to contact the office. Additional information can only be released upon receipt of signed authorization from the patient.

Sincerely,

Alvin Trotter, M.D.

Jul 28 21, 07:02p STENSON TOLAN 323-643-4208 p.1

```
1/05/04 11:11:11 WC N BANK LEVY|ECG          , BOOK
5/10/04 09:09:09 DBT CHG CRT: 208.00|IV
5/11/04 10:10:10 DBT CHG CRT: 240.00|IV
5/28/04 15:15:15 BNK LEVY SRVED 5/20/04 NO FUNDS AVAILABLE|IV
5/07/04 14:14:14 DBT CHG CRT: 270.00|JS
5/22/04 16:16:16 COE GRANTED WE TO GET 75.00 PER PAY PERIOD & ALL
5/22/04 16:16:16        MONIES HELD WL BE RELEASED TO PCX|IV
5/16/05 14:14:14 SC# 9450|ECG
1/23/06 15:15:15 SC# 1601 N LONG BEACH|JW
1/14/06 13:13:13 SC# 9450|ECG
7/31/07 15:15:15 ......DTR WILL BE ABLE TO STL ACCT FOR 5K TOM WILL
7/31/07 15:15:15  WELLSFARGO IT|ECG
8/02/07 14:14:14 F. RUBIO 3108845777WELLS DTR $5000 CASH|JC
8/02/07 14:14:14 CALL HDQT AT 2.45PM WILL NOT CONFIRM TRANS|JC
8/02/07 15:15:15 ...AGREED TO STL ACCT 4 5K|ECG
8/03/07 08:08:08 WIP REMOVED, ZERO BALANCE ACCT
9/19/07 11:11:11 AL FOLDER RET AS PD|JS
0/13/73 99:99:99 EXP(042705U) TUN(042705U) CBI(042705U)
2/27/98 00:00:00 Letter 001 Sent
3/05/98 12:12:12 CLD BAGOT DTR. ON LINE GAVE TO LISA.|JT
3/05/98 12:12:12 AUTOMATIC MAIL STOPPED|LIS
3/05/98 12:12:12 UN C FR:2   TO 2P|LIS
3/05/98 12:12:12 WP C FR:000-0000000|LIS
3/05/98 12:12:12 DTR AGREED TO $150 EA 13TH ST 3/13/98. SENT NOTE.|
3/05/98 12:12:12 LIS
3/18/98 16:16:16 TT DTR BA. SZ NOTE NOT RECD. ADV DTR WILL RESEND T
3/18/98 16:16:16 ODAY.SZ HE WILL CB, CAN'T TALK. I RESENT NOTE.|LIS
3/24/98 00:00:00 Letter 011 Sent
4/08/98 14:14:14 UN C FR:2P  TO 2PS|LIS
4/08/98 14:14:14 IN ASSET BOX....|LIS
5/01/98 09:09:09 IN SUIT BOX.....|LIS
6/05/98 10:10:10 UN C FR:2PS TO 2L|JS
6/05/98 10:10:10 IN FOR SUIT|JS
7/02/98 09:09:09 PER 'AAS' BILL S/C'D @ B/A 6-28 $30 MM
7/14/98 16:16:16 SC# 98C01454 MM
7/14/98 16:16:16 SC# 9801454 MM
7/14/98 16:16:16 DBT CHG PRIN: 6029.41 INTA:   18.17 CRT:     .00 A
7/14/98 16:16:16 TTY:       .00 MM
7/29/98 15:15:15 S/C'D @ B/A 6-26-98.. MM
7/29/98 15:15:15 DBT CHG CRT:   90.00 MM
7/29/98 15:15:15 ACCT TO LISA....MM
7/30/98 08:08:08 LM BA FOR DTR. TO LEGALS FOR AFFID....|LIS
7/30/98 13:13:13 DTR 0 OFF MSSG. AGREED TO STIP $150 EA 21ST ST 8/2
7/30/98 13:13:13 1/98.TO LEGALS FOR STIP...|LIS
9/04/98 09:09:09 09:07:46 996 NOTICE REQUESTED     82198   150.00|L
9/04/98 09:09:09 IS
9/04/98 09:09:09 LM BA|LIS
9/08/98 00:00:00 Letter 996 Sent
12/17/98 10:10:10 MELA TO WK W/COURT ON 'J' STATUS.|LIS
12/17/98 10:10:10 SENT LETTER TO COURT REQUESTING STATUS ON "J" MM
12/17/98 10:10:10 IN COURT CALL BOX. MM
03/17/99 14:14:14 ACCT TO MELA SEEN THAT W/C WAS PUT BACK WITHOUT WO
03/17/99 14:14:14 RKINGTHE "J"|AA
```

#5 THIS GO IN THE BOOK

authorized capacity(ies), and that by his/her/their signature(s) on the instrument the person(s), or the entity upon behalf of which the person(s) acted, executed the instrument

WITNESS my hand and official seal

ADRIANA I. RAMOS
Commission # 1617681
Notary Public - California
Los Angeles County
My Comm. Expires Nov 1, 2009

NOTARY SEAL

NOTARY SIGNATURE

Adriana I Ramos
(Typed Name of Notary)

Page of 03.01.00 (04/08)

Los Angeles Police Department
INVESTIGATIVE REPORT

☐ COMBINED EVID REPORT
☐ MULTIPLE DRS ON THIS REPORT

REPORT OF:	[illegible]
INVEST DIV.	77th
INC #	[illegible]
DR #	[illegible]

CASE SCREENING FACTOR(S)

- ☒ SUSPECT/VEHICLE NOT SEEN
- ☐ PRINTS OR OTHER EVIDENCE NOT PRESENT
- ☒ MO NOT DISTINCT
- ☒ PROPERTY LOSS LESS THAN $5,000
- ☒ NO SERIOUS INJURY TO VICTIM
- ☒ ONLY ONE VICTIM INVOLVED

VICTIM

LAST NAME, FIRST, MIDDLE (OR NAME OF BUSINESS)	SEX	DESC	HT	WT	AGE	DOB
[illegible] STINSON G	M	BLK	5'	150	66	07-23-43

ADDRESS	ZIP	PHONE
R- 1539 W. 94th St. L A	90047	(323) 373-0530
B-		248-6274

DR. LIC. NO. (IF NONE, OTHER ID & NO.): J091 0537
FOREIGN LANGUAGE SPOKEN (IF APPLICABLE): —
OCCUPATION: Retired

PREMISES (SPECIFIC TYPE) ☐ ATM: Residence

ENTRY AREA/POINT OF ENTRY — POINT OF EXIT
☐ FRONT ☐ REAR ☐ SIDE ☐ ROOF ☐ FLOOR ☐ OTHER

METHOD

INSTRUMENT/TOOL USED

LOCATION OF OCCURRENCE — SAME AS VS ☒ RES. ☐ BUS. — R.D. 1263

PRINTS BY PREL. INV. ATTEMPT ☐ Y ☒ N — OBTAINED ☐ Y ☒ N

DATE & TIME OF OCCURRENCE: 09-14-07 0930

DATE & TIME REPORTED TO PD: 10-08-09 1200

TYPE PROPERTY STOLEN/LOST/DAMAGED ☐ 12.04.03 G VEN: [illegible] - Property — STOLEN/LOST: $ — — RECOVERED: $ — — EST. DAMAGED ARSON/VAND.: $ —

VICT'S VEH. (IF INVOLVED) YEAR, MAKE, TYPE, COLOR, LIC. NO.

NOTIFICATION(S) (PERSON & DIVISION): —

CONNECTED REPORT(S) (TYPE & DR #): —

MO IF LONG FORM, LIST UNIQUE ACTIONS. IF SHORT FORM, DESCRIBE SUSPECT'S ACTIONS IN BRIEF PHRASES, INCLUDING WEAPON USED. DO NOT REPEAT ABOVE INFO BUT CLARIFY REPORT AS NECESSARY. IF ANY OF THE MISSING ITEMS ARE POTENTIALLY IDENTIFIABLE, ITEMIZE AND DESCRIBE ALL ITEMS MISSING IN THIS INCIDENT IN THE NARRATIVE.

Susp.(s) Forged Vict's Name [illegible] to a Notarize Document. Mansion [illegible] Given

SUSPICIOUS ACTIVITY(SAR) ☐ HATE CRIME/INCIDENT ☐ DOMESTIC VIOLENCE ☐

REPORTING EMPLOYEE(S)	INITIALS, LAST NAME	SERIAL NO.	DIV./DETAIL
	Russom, Jc.	26997	77th
			[illegible]

PERSON REPORTING — SIGNATURE — DR RECEIVED BY PHONE ☐

NOTE: IF SHORT FORM AND VICTIM/PR ARE NOT THE SAME, ENTER PR INFORMATION IN INVOLVED PERSONS SECTION.

THIS REPORT DOES NOT CONSTITUTE VALID IDENTIFICATION

KEEP THIS REPORT FOR REFERENCE. INSTRUCCIONES EN ESPANOL AL REVERSO.

Your case will be assigned to a detective for follow-up investigation based upon specific facts obtained during the initial investigation. Studies have shown that the presence of these facts can predict whether a detailed follow-up investigation would likely result in the arrest and prosecution of the suspect(s) or the recovery of property, in a manner that is cost-effective to you, the taxpayer. Significant decreases in personnel have made it impossible for detectives to personally discuss each and every case with all crime victims. A detective will not routinely contact you, unless the detective requires additional information.

TO REPORT ADDITIONAL INFORMATION: If you have specific facts to provide which might assist in the investigation of your case, please contact the detective Monday through Friday, between 8:00 A.M. and 9:30 P.M., or between 2:30 P.M. and 4:00 P.M. at telephone number ______________. If the detective is not available when you call, please leave a message and include the telephone number where you can be reached.

COPY OF REPORT: If you wish to purchase a copy of the complete report, phone (213) 485-4193 to obtain the purchase price. Send a check or money order payable to the Los Angeles Police Department to Records and Identification Division, Box 30158, Los Angeles, CA 90030. Include a copy of this report or the following information with your request: 1) Name and address of victims; 2) Type of report and DR number (if listed above); 3) Date and location of occurrence. NOTE: Requests not accompanied by proper payment will not be processed.

DR NUMBER: If not entered on this form, the DR number may be obtained by writing to Records and Identification Division and giving the information needed to obtain a copy of the report (see above paragraph). Specify that you only want the DR number. It will be forwarded without delay. There is no charge for this service.

CREDIT CARDS/CHECKS: Immediately notify concerned credit corporation or banks to avoid possibility of being liable for someone else using your stolen or lost credit card or check.

HOW YOU CAN HELP THE INVESTIGATION OF YOUR CASE:
* Keep this memo for reference.
* If stolen items have serial numbers not available at time of report, attempt to locate them and phone them to the detective at the listed number.
* If you discover additional losses, complete and mail in the Supplemental Property Loss form given to you by the reporting employee.
* Promptly report recovery of property.
* Promptly report additional information such as a neighbor informing you of suspicious activity at time crime occurred.

VICTIM-WITNESS ASSISTANCE PROGRAM: The Los Angeles City and County Victim-Witness Assistance Program (VWAP) can help to determine if you qualify for Victim of Violent Crime compensation. If you qualify, they will assist with filling your claim application. If you are a victim or a witness to a crime and will be going to court, they will explain the court procedures to you. Their staff may also assist you with other problems created by the crime.

To find the program location nearest to you, call the Victim-Witness Assistance Program at the Los Angeles City Attorney's Office (213) 485-6976, or the Los Angeles County District Attorney's Office (213) 974-7499.

VICTIMS OF VIOLENT CRIME COMPENSATION: Refer to paragraph at bottom of reverse side.

www.LAPDOnline.org
www.joinLAPD.com

3

as borrowers, for a revolving line of credit account (the "Agreement"), as well as any modifications and renewals of the Agreement. The Agreement provides for a Total Credit Commitment (as defined in the Agreement) of $ 60,000.00 , allows for repeated credit advances drawn against the Total Credit Commitment, and provides for a variable interest rate. By mutual agreement, Bank may increase the Total Credit Commitment ("Increased Credit Commitment"), and

- Trustor's performance of each obligation in this Deed of Trust

This Deed of Trust will not secure borrowers' obligations under the Agreement in excess of the Total Credit Commitment or Increased Credit Commitment, except for any amounts due to (a) unpaid interest, or (b) expenses that Bank incurs because obligations of a borrower under the Agreement are not fulfilled (including without limitation, any advances that Bank makes to perform borrowers' duties to pay taxes, insurance, etc.)

To Protect the Security of this Deed of Trust, I Agree: By the execution and delivery of this Deed of Trust and the Equity Maximizer Agreement and Disclosure secured hereby, that provisions (3) to (20), inclusive of the fictitious deed of trust recorded in LOS ANGELES County JULY 19, 1999 , as Instrument No 99-1334924 in Book and at Page of the Official Records of the County Recorder of that county, (which provisions, identical in all counties, are printed on the following pages) hereby are adopted and incorporated herein and made a part hereof as though set forth at length, and I will observe and perform such provisions, and that the reference to Property, obligations, and parties in such provisions shall be construed to refer to the Property, obligations, and parties set forth in this Deed of Trust

Trustor requests that a copy of **ANY NOTICE OF DEFAULT AND ANY NOTICE OF SALE** under this Deed of Trust be mailed to Trustor at the Trustor's address shown below, or if no address is shown, then at the address of the Property

Mailing Address for Notices 1539 W 94TH ST, LOS ANGELES, CALIFORNIA
90047-3913

BY SIGNING BELOW, Trustor accepts and agrees to the terms and covenants contained in this Security Instrument and in any Rider executed by Trustor and recorded with it

Stenson E. Tolan (Seal)
STENSON E TOLAN -Trustor

_______________ (Seal) -Trustor

_______________ (Seal) -Trustor

_______________ (Seal) -Trustor

_______________ (Seal) -Trustor

_______________ (Seal) -Trustor

STENSON E TOLAN/9950719916211C0
CALIFORNIA SHORT FORM DEED OF TRUST
(EQUITY MAXIMIZER ACCOUNT)
CAHESISF BOA 02/02/07

Page 2 of 3

DocMagic eForms 800-649-1362
www.docmagic.com

Jul 26 21, 07:11p STENSON TOLAN 323-643-4208 p.4

401 EAST MANCHESTER BLVD., SUITE 209
INGLEWOOD, CALIFORNIA 90301
678-3233

INSTRUCTIONS
Page 1

THIS DOCUMENT WILL AFFECT YOUR LEGAL RIGHTS – READ IT CAREFULLY!

Escrow Number 1282-DM

Date July 6, 1977 Escrow Officer Pat Morrill

Purchaser will hand you sufficient funds to cover closing costs $ 600.00

and cash down payment of: $ 26,900.00

Proceeds from first trust deed loan to be procured by purchaser FHA 203-B $

TOTAL CONSIDERATION $ 27,500.00

Any additional funds and instruments required from either purchasers or sellers will be handed you to enable you to comply with these instructions, which you are to use on or before August 6, 19 77, and when you can obtain a Standard Policy of Title Insurance with a liability of $ 27,500.00

on real property in the city and County of Los Angeles State of California,

Commonly known as: 1539 West 94th Street, Los Angeles, California

Legally described as: Lot 549 of Tract 6084

of maps, in the office of

as per map recorded in book 101 page(s) 53-57

the County Recorder of said County, State of California, except any oil or mineral reservations of record

Show title vested in: STENSON E. TOLAN, Jr. and LOIS TOLAN, Husband and Wife as Joint Tenants

Free of encumbrance except:

(A) 1977/1978 general county and city, if any, and special taxes for the current fiscal year; includi any special district levies, payments for which are included therein and collected therewith. A lien not yet payable.

(B) EASEMENTS, rights of way, conditions, restrictions, and reservations of record.

(C) Deed of Trust securing a note for $ 26,900.00 dated during escrow in favor of any FHA/HU approved mortgagee, with interest from date of disbursement at the then prevailing rate, as authorized by FHA/HU prior to recording the deed of trust. PURCHASERS EXECUTION OF LOAN DOCUMENTS EVIDENC APPROVAL OF SAME AS TO FORM AND CONTENT. Further, you are to comply with the instructions of t lender.

You are to charge the purchasers with down payment, if any, and with the costs of obtaining new loan, includ but not limited to, ALTA policy fee, recording fees, credit report, tax service, impounds for taxes, hazard insura and mutual mortgage insurance, 1% loan origination fee and purchasers escrow fee.

Purchasers to furnish new hazard insurance coverage as per lenders requirements and pay for same. Existing pol if received in escrow, is to be forwarded to the sellers at the close of escrow, for their disposition.

You are to charge the sellers with lenders loan discount fee AS REQUIRED for the new loan being obtaine purchasers and all loan origination fees of FHA/HUD and/or lender not chargeable to purchasers as per len instructions and balance of purchasers escrow fee.

Sellers to deposit in escrow for the purchasers a pest control report of recent date from a licensed pest co operator showing subject property to be free of visible evidence of termite, dry rot and fungus and in compl with FHA/HUD regulations. From the funds accruing to the sellers at the close of escrow, you are authoriz pay for same in the event you are handed a bill.

It is expressly agreed, that, notwithstanding any other provisions of this contract, the purchaser shall not be gated to complete the purchase of the property described herein or to incur any penalty by forfeiture of e money deposits or otherwise unless the seller has delivered to the purchaser a written statement by the F Housing Commissioner setting forth the appraised value of the property for mortgage insurance purposes less than $ 27,500.00, not including closing costs which statem seller hereby agrees to deliver to the purchaser promptly after such appraised value statement is made avail the seller. The purchaser shall, however, have the privilege and option of proceeding with the consummation contract without regard to the amount of the appraised valuation by the Federal Housing Commissioner.

From the funds deposited in escrow for the credit of the purchasers, you are authorized to pay for the appra the credit report forthwith, upon demand, regardless of the consummation of escrow, charging buyers for appraisal and charging buyers for the credit report at the close of escrow.

based on the latest figures available to you,

Lot 10 of the West Adams and Western Avenue Tract, in the City of Los Angeles, State of California, as per map recorded in Book 6 Page 1 of Maps, in the Office of the County Recorder of said county.

State of Califor

Commonly known as 2115 W. 28th Street, Los Angeles, CA 90018.

This conveyance transfers the grantor's interest into her revocable trust and is exempt from transfer tax under R&T Code §11911.

DATED: 7-12-02

STATE OF CALIFORNIA
COUNTY OF Los ANGELES
ON July 12 2002 before me, personally appeared HELEN M. DAVIS personally known to me (or proved to me on the basis of satisfactory evidence) to be the person(s) whose name(s) is/are subscribed to the within instrument and acknowledged to me that he/she/they executed the same in his/her/their authorized capacity(ies), and that by his/her/their signature(s) on the instrument the person(s), or the entity upon behalf of which the person(s) acted, executed the instrument.

Witness my hand and official seal.

Signature Sandra Nixon, Notary Public

HELEN M. DAVIS
Helen M. Davis

Signed by Edward M. Abounasse For Helen M. Davis

SANDRA NIXON
Commission # 1281484
Notary Public — California
Los Angeles County
My Comm. Expires May 18, 2004

MAIL TAX STATEMENT AS DIRECTED ABOVE

ATD-13F (Rev 4/94)

QUITCLAIM DEED

JURISDICTION

6. On or about January 29, 2001 (the Petition Date"), Cross-Plaintiff, Tolan filed for relief under Chapter 7 of the Bankruptcy Code. Thereafter, David A. Gill was appointed as the Chapter 7 Trustee for the Tolan estate.

7. The Tolan Bankruptcy Case was closed as a no asset case pursuant to an order entered on or about May 31, 2001.

8. The Tolan Bankruptcy Case was re-opened pursuant to an order entered on August 13, 2007 on the Trustee's motion. Thereafter, the Trustee was re-appointed as Trustee for the Tolan Bankruptcy Case.

9. This action is a core proceeding and this Court has jurisdiction pursuant to 28 U.S.C. §§ 157 (A), (B), (E), (N) and (O), 1334 (b), Rule 7001 (4) of the Federal Rules of Bankruptcy Procedure.

2

authorized capacity(ies), and that by his/her/their signature(s) on the instrument the person(s), or the entity upon behalf of which the person(s) acted, executed the instrument

WITNESS my hand and official seal

ADRIANA I. RAMOS
Commission # 1617681
Notary Public - California
Los Angeles County
My Comm. Expires Nov 1, 2009

NOTARY SEAL

Adriana I. Ramos
NOTARY SIGNATURE

Adriana I. Ramos
(Typed Name of Notary)

Page 1 of 03.01.00 (04/38)

Los Angeles Police Department
INVESTIGATIVE REPORT

☐ COMBINED EVID REPORT
☐ MULTIPLE DRS ON THIS REPORT

CASE SCREENING FACTOR(S)

- ☒ SUSPECT/VEHICLE NOT SEEN
- ☐ PRINTS OR OTHER EVIDENCE NOT PRESENT
- ☒ MO NOT DISTINCT
- ☒ PROPERTY LOSS LESS THAN $5,000
- ☒ NO SERIOUS INJURY TO VICTIM
- ☐ ONLY ONE VICTIM INVOLVED

REPORT OF: - 3RE-GERY

RPT DIST DIV.: 77th | DR #: 09-120801 | DIV #: 09-12

VICTIM

LAST NAME, FIRST, MIDDLE (OR NAME OF BUSINESS): ... LAND STEVENSON G | SEX: M | DESC: BLK | HT: 5'11 | WT: 193 | AGE: 66 | DOB: 07-23-43

ADDRESS R: 1539 W. 94th st. L A 90047 | PHONE (323) 373-0536

ADDRESS B: | ZIP | PHONE 323 248-6274

DR. LIC. NO. (IF NONE, OTHER ID & NO.): J0910537 | FOREIGN LANGUAGE SPOKEN (IF APPLICABLE): — | OCCUPATION: Retired

PREMISES (SPECIFIC TYPE): Residence ☐ ATM

ENTRY (SPECIFY POINT OF ENTRY) ☐ FRONT ☐ REAR ☐ SIDE ☐ ROOF ☐ FLOOR ☐ OTHER | POINT OF EXIT

METHOD:

INSTRUMENT/TOOL USED:

LOCATION OF OCCURRENCE: SAME AS VR ☒ RES. ☐ BUS. | R.D. 1263 | PRINTS BY PREL. INV. ATTEMPT ☐ Y ☒ N OBTAINED ☐ Y ☒ N

DATE & TIME OF OCCURRENCE: 08-14-02 0900 | DATE & TIME REPORTED TO PD: 10-08-09 1200

TYPE PROPERTY STOLEN/LOST/DAMAGED: Identity - Property | STOLEN/LOST $ — | RECOVERED $ — | EST. DAMAGED ARSON/VAND. $ —

VICT'S VEH. (IF INVOLVED) YEAR, MAKE, TYPE, COLOR, LIC. NO.: | NOTIFICATION(S) (PERSON & DIVISION): — | CONNECTED REPORT(S) (TYPE & DR #):

MO IF LONG FORM, LIST UNIQUE ACTIONS. IF SHORT FORM, DESCRIBE SUSPECT'S ACTIONS IN BRIEF PHRASES, INCLUDING WEAPON USED. DO NOT REPEAT ABOVE INFO BUT CLARIFY REPORT AS NECESSARY. IF ANY OF THE MISSING ITEMS ARE POTENTIALLY IDENTIFIABLE, ITEMIZE AND DESCRIBE ALL ITEMS MISSING IN THIS INCIDENT & THE NARRATIVE.

Susp.(s) Forging Vict's Name on to a notarize Document. Mansen's Law Given

SUSPICIOUS ACTIVITY(SAR) ☐ | HATE CRIME/INCIDENT ☐ | DOMESTIC VIOLENCE ☐

REPORTING EMPLOYEE(S): INITIALS, LAST NAME: Russom, Jc. | SERIAL NO.: 26557 | DIV/DETAIL: 77th / Desk | PERSON REPORTING SIGNATURE: [signature] Jr. | DR RECEIVED BY PHONE ☐

NOTE: IF SHORT FORM AND VICTIM/PR ARE NOT THE SAME, ENTER PR INFORMATION IN INVOLVED PERSONS SECTION.

THIS REPORT DOES NOT CONSTITUTE VALID IDENTIFICATION

KEEP THIS REPORT FOR REFERENCE. INSTRUCCIONES EN ESPANOL AL REVERSO.

Your case will be assigned to a detective for follow-up investigation based upon specific facts obtained during the initial investigation. Studies have shown that the presence of these facts can predict whether a detailed follow-up investigation would likely result in the arrest and prosecution of the suspect(s) or the recovery of property, in a manner that is cost-effective to you, the taxpayer. Significant decreases in personnel have made it impossible for detectives to personally discuss each and every case with all crime victims. A detective will not routinely contact you, unless the detective requires additional information.

TO REPORT ADDITIONAL INFORMATION: If you have specific facts to provide which might assist in the investigation of your case, please contact the detective Monday through Friday, between 8:00 A.M. and 9:30 P.M., or between 2:30 P.M. and 4:00 P.M. at telephone number __________. If the detective is not available when you call, please leave a message and include the telephone number where you can be reached.

COPY OF REPORT: If you wish to purchase a copy of the complete report, phone (213) 485-4193 to obtain the purchase price. Send a check or money order payable to the Los Angeles Police Department to Records and Identification Division, Box 30158, Los Angeles, CA 90030. Include a copy of this report or the following information with your request: 1) Name and address of victims; 2) Type of report and DR number (if listed above); 3) Date and location of occurrence. NOTE: Requests not accompanied by proper payment will not be processed.

DR NUMBER: If not entered on this form, the DR number may be obtained by writing to Records and Identification Division and giving the information needed to obtain a copy of the report (see above paragraph). Specify that you only want the DR number. It will be forwarded without delay. There is no charge for this service.

CREDIT CARDS/CHECKS: Immediately notify concerned credit corporation or banks to avoid possibility of being liable for someone else using your stolen or lost credit card or check.

HOW YOU CAN HELP THE INVESTIGATION OF YOUR CASE:

* Keep this memo for reference.
* If stolen items have serial numbers not available at time of report, attempt to locate them and phone them to the detective at the listed number.
* If you discover additional losses, complete and mail in the Supplemental Property Loss form given to you by the reporting employee.
* Promptly report recovery of property.
* Promptly report additional information such as a neighbor informing you of suspicious activity at time crime occurred.

VICTIM-WITNESS ASSISTANCE PROGRAM: The Los Angeles City and County Victim-Witness Assistance Program (VWAP) can help to determine if you qualify for Victim of Violent Crime compensation. If you qualify, they will assist with filing your claim application. If you are a victim or a witness to a crime and will be going to court, they will explain the court procedures to you. Their staff may also assist you with other problems created by the crime.

To find the program location nearest to you, call the Victim-Witness Assistance Program at the Los Angeles City Attorney's Office (213) 485-6976, or the Los Angeles County District Attorney's Office (213) 974-7499.

VICTIMS OF VIOLENT CRIME COMPENSATION: Refer to paragraph at bottom of reverse side.

www.LAPDOnline.org
www.joinLAPD.com

DR NO 06033 8214

470 WEST 55TH

WELLSFARGO

SUSPECT OBTAINED HIS ACCOUNT INFORMATION $550.00
EVIDENCE FINANCIAL INSTITUTION PROVIDED CAMERA

BANKRUPTCY COURT 01-29-01

STANLEY TOLAN
565-58-7546
1264 WEST 64TH
LA CA 90044

CLERK OF COURT JON D. CERETTO 01-26-01
269,250 UNSECURED $807,750
DEPUTY CLERK 213-894-4981 DONNA Johnson
LA01

DAVE GEL
EDWARD
ABOUNASSAR

FRAUD
QUITCLAIM DEED
CASE NUMBER# 201-

CIT/CASE: BC585905
LEA/DEF#:

RECEIPT #: CCH195707057
DATE PAID: 08/06/15 03:33 PM
PAYMENT: $20.00
RECEIVED:
CHECK: $20.00
CASH: $0.00
CHANGE: $0.00
CARD: $0.00

310

08/21/2015

SUPERIOR COURT OF THE STATE OF CALIFORNIA

COUNTY OF LOS ANGELES, CENTRAL DISTRICT

ROSIO VARGAS, an individual; and JOSE VARGAS, an individual,

Plaintiffs,

v.

STANLEY TOLAN AKA STENLEY TOLAN, an individual; STENSON E. TOLAN, an individual; and Does 1 through 10, inclusive,

Defendants.

Case No. BC585905

STIPULATION FOR ENTRY OF JUDGMENT, AND [PROPOSED] JUDGMENT

Judge: Hon. Deirdre Hill
Dept: 49

Complaint Filed: June 22, 2015

Stenson E. Tolan Jr./II

Client Statement
the Leone Law Group

April 1, 2012 – April 30, 2012

Date	Attorney Service(s) Provided	Time Devoted
April 5 2012	Client Interview	25 minutes
April 10 2012	Reviewed Property Documents Obtained from County Recorder	1 hour 30 minutes
	Follow-Up Calls for Client Medical Files	
April 18 2012	Drafted Pre-Litigation Case Report, Case Timeline, and List of Potential Witnesses and Defendants	1 hour 10 minutes
April 24 2012	Drafted/Revised Pre-Litigation Report, Case Timeline, and List of Potential Witnesses and Defendants	3 hours 15 minutes
Various Dates	Phone Calls to/from Client	Not Charged on this Statement
Subtotal Attorney Time - 6.3 hours x $200/hr		$1,260
Expense		Cost
mileage		$7.77
10% administrative fee per fee agreement		$126.00
Subtotal Expenses		$133.77
Total Due for This Statement Period		$1,393.77
Amount Due from Last Statement		$717.24
Payment Received Since Last Statement		$1,000.00
Balance – Amount Now Due		$1,111.01

Remit payment to:

Damian Leone
the Leone Law Group
10100 Santa Monica Blvd. Third Floor
Century City, CA 90067

Jul 26 21, 07:02p STENSON TOLAN 323-643-4208 p.2

(310) 671-5353

Internal Medicine

October 19, 2015

To: Whom it may concern

Fr: Alvin Trotter, M.D.

Re: Stinson *Tolan*

Mr. Tolan is a long-term patient of mine. Mr. Tolan told me that his son had taken his house and that he had borrowed $60.000.00 against his house. He is under a great deal of stress due to this matter between him and his son.

Mr. Tolan has reported multiple issues with his son he is stressed due to the loss of his home. He states he had no understanding that paperwork he signed would cause the loss of his home.

If you have any questions, or need additional information, please feel free to contact the office. Additional information can only be released upon receipt of signed authorization from the patient.

Sincerely,

Alvin Trotter, M.D.

PARTIES

1. Cross/Plaintiff Stanley Tolan ("Tolan") is the debtor in above-captioned Chapter 7 case (the "Tolan Bankruptcy Case") .

2. Cross-Defendant David A. Gill is the Chapter 7 Trustee (the "Tolan Trustee").

3. Cross-Plaintiff is informed and believes, and based thereon alleges, that Edward and Aida Abounassar are debtors in bankruptcy, having filed a joint voluntary petition for relief under Chapter 7 of the Bankruptcy Code on or about July 11, 2007, bearing Case No.: 2:07-bk-15328-EC (the "Abounassar Bankruptcy case") .

4. Cross-Plaintiff is informed and believes, and based thereon alleges, that cross-defendant Timothy J. Yoo ("Yoo") is the Chapter 7 Trustee in the Abounassar Bankruptcy Case.

5. Cross-Plaintiff is informed and believes, and based thereon alleges, that cross-defendant Washington Bank, ("WAMU") is a bank and/or federal association ("WAMU") is authorized to transact business in the State of California .

JURISDICTION

6. On or about January 29, 2001 (the Petition Date"), Cross-Plaintiff, Tolan filed for relief under Chapter 7 of the Bankruptcy Code. Thereafter, David A. Gill was appointed as the Chapter 7 Trustee for the Tolan estate.

7. The Tolan Bankruptcy Case was closed as a no asset case pursuant to an order entered on or about May 31, 2001.

8. The Tolan Bankruptcy Case was re-opened pursuant to an order entered on August 13, 2007 on the Trustee's motion. Thereafter, the Trustee was re-appointed as Trustee for the Tolan Bankruptcy Case.

9. This action is a core proceeding and this Court has jurisdiction pursuant to 28 U.S.C. §§ 157 (A), (B), (E), (N) and (O), 1334 (b), Rule 7001 (4) of the Federal Rules of Bankruptcy Procedure.

2

IN ME BOOK

CHIEF COMPLAINT: Nausea and vomiting.

HISTORY OF PRESENT ILLNESS: Helen is an 83-year-old female who was brought into the emergency room by paramedics after she had been complaining of dizziness, and was found to be hypertensive. Initial blood pressure was 245/80 in the emergency room, and by paramedics in the field it had been 184/110. The patient does not recall her home medications, but states that she had not been taking her medications because she was not feeling well. On further questioning she denies any syncope or nausea, apart from described above. No other episodes of emesis except for above. No diarrhea. No abdominal pain. No other GI or GU complaints. No chest pain, hemoptysis, night sweats or weight loss.

PAST MEDICAL HISTORY:
1. Hypertension.
2. Previous cerebrovascular accident.

MEDICATIONS AT HOME: Pills for hypertension; names unknown.

ALLERGIES: NONE.

PREVIOUS SURGERY: Hysterectomy.

SOCIAL HISTORY: The patient lives by herself. She states she has an adopted son called Stanley who is going to be living with her, but at this time she still lives by herself.

PHYSICAL EXAMINATION:

GENERAL: Elderly female.

VITAL SIGNS: Blood pressure at this time 180/110, respirations 18, heart rate 84, afebrile.

HEENT: Exam unremarkable. There is no facial asymmetry. Tongue midline. Gag intact. Pupils equal, round, reactive to light and accommodation.

NECK: Supple. No JVD or thyromegaly.

CHEST: Exam shows clear breath sounds bilaterally.

HEART: Normal heart tones. S1 and S2 without murmurs.

PUT THIS FOR STANLEY TSLAM

MIDWAY HOSPITAL MEDICAL CENTER
5925 SAN VICENTE BOULEVARD
LOS ANGELES, CALIFORNIA 90019
(323) 938-3161

PATIENT: DAVIS, HELEN
MED. REC #: 28-21-44
PT. NUM #: 102784469
ROOM #: 3062
ATT. PHYS: SYED OMAR TIRMIZI, M.D.
ADMIT DATE: 05/30/2001

PAGE 1 of

HISTORY AND PHYSICAL
PRINTED BY: AGONZALEZ
DATE 1/10/2007

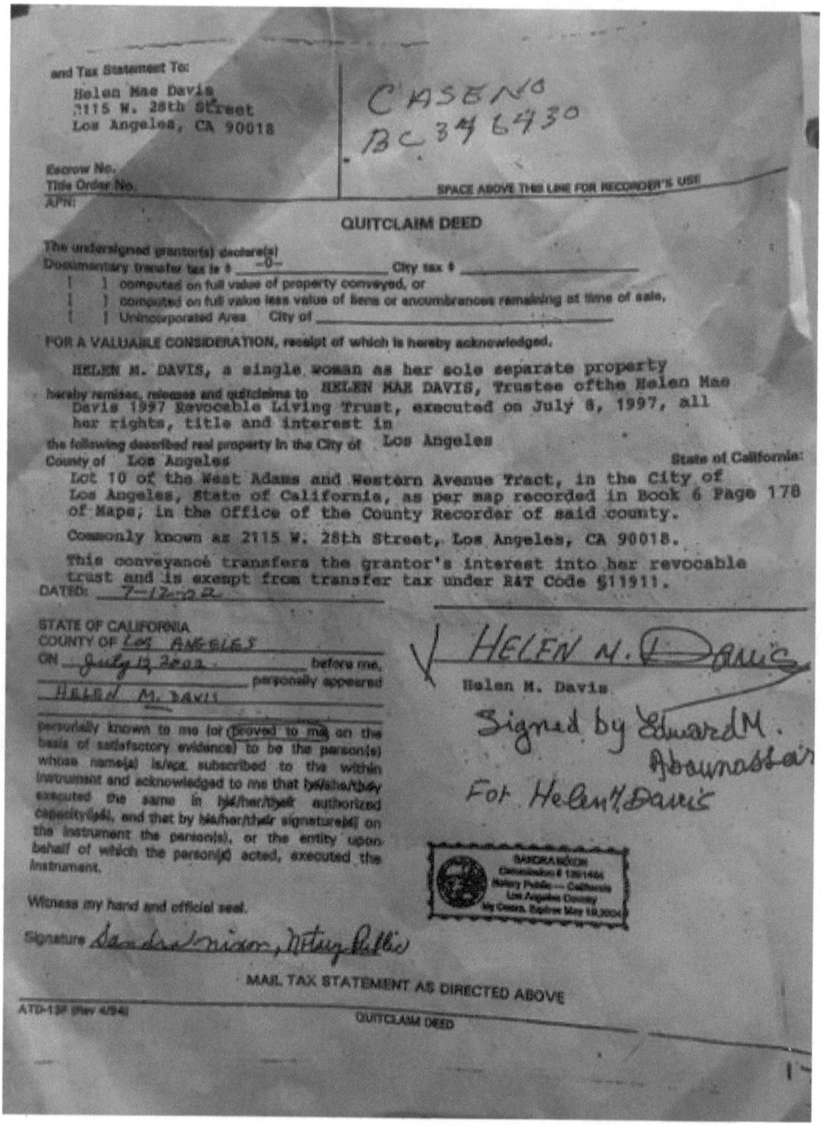

and Tax Statement To:

Helen Mae Davis
2115 W. 28th Street
Los Angeles, CA 90018

CASE NO
BC 346430

Escrow No.
Title Order No.
APN:

SPACE ABOVE THIS LINE FOR RECORDER'S USE

QUITCLAIM DEED

The undersigned grantor(s) declare(s)
Documentary transfer tax is $ -0- City tax $
[ ] computed on full value of property conveyed, or
[ ] computed on full value less value of liens or encumbrances remaining at time of sale,
[ ] Unincorporated Area City of

FOR A VALUABLE CONSIDERATION, receipt of which is hereby acknowledged,

HELEN M. DAVIS, a single woman as her sole separate property

hereby remises, releases and quitclaims to HELEN MAE DAVIS, Trustee ofthe Helen Mae Davis 1997 Revocable Living Trust, executed on July 8, 1997, all her rights, title and interest in

the following described real property in the City of Los Angeles
County of Los Angeles State of California:

Lot 10 of the West Adams and Western Avenue Tract, in the City of Los Angeles, State of California, as per map recorded in Book 6 Page 178 of Maps, in the Office of the County Recorder of said county.

Commonly known as 2115 W. 28th Street, Los Angeles, CA 90018.

This conveyance transfers the grantor's interest into her revocable trust and is exempt from transfer tax under R&T Code §11911.

DATED: 7-12-02

STATE OF CALIFORNIA
COUNTY OF Los Angeles
ON July 12 2002 before me,
personally appeared
HELEN M. DAVIS

personally known to me (or proved to me on the basis of satisfactory evidence) to be the person(s) whose name(s) is/are subscribed to the within instrument and acknowledged to me that he/she/they executed the same in his/her/their authorized capacity(ies), and that by his/her/their signature(s) on the instrument the person(s), or the entity upon behalf of which the person(s) acted, executed the instrument.

Witness my hand and official seal.

Signature Sandra Nixon, Notary Public

HELEN M. DAVIS
Helen M. Davis
Signed by Edward M. Abounassar
For Helen M. Davis

SANDRA NIXON
Commission # 1261464
Notary Public — California
Los Angeles County
My Comm. Expires May 18, 2004

MAIL TAX STATEMENT AS DIRECTED ABOVE

ATD-13P (Rev 4/94) QUITCLAIM DEED

(213) 974-4144
Fax: (213) 687-1137
e-mail: rsaenz@dca.lacounty.gov

RUDY SAENZ
Investigator
Department of Consumer Affairs

County of Los Angeles
Kenneth Hahn Hall of Administration

500 W. Temple Street, B96
Los Angeles, CA 90012

JEFFREY PRANG
ASSESSOR

EL CID DE RAMUS
Office of the Assessor

EDeramus@assessor.lacounty.gov
213-974-3101

Ph: 213-893-1478

Rosalva ~~Luna~~ Dubón
Supervisor
rdubon@ttc.lacounty.gov

225 N. Hill Street
Kenneth Hahn Hall of Administration
Room 122
Los Angeles, CA 90012

Treasurer and Tax Collector
County of Los Angeles

Ph: 213-893-~~1478~~ 1474

Rosalva ~~Luna~~ Dubón
Supervisor
rdubon@ttc.lacounty.gov

225 N. Hill Street
Kenneth Hahn Hall of Administration
Room 122
Los Angeles, CA 90012

Treasurer and Tax Collector
County of Los Angeles

---

(213) 974-4144
Fax: (213) 687-1137
e-mail: rsaenz@dca.lacounty.gov

RUDY SAENZ
Investigator
Department of Consumer Affairs

County of Los Angeles
Kenneth Hahn Hall of Administration

500 W. Temple Street, B96
Los Angeles, CA 90012

About the Author

Stenson Edward Tolan is a hardworking man who invested his prime working at various and distinct corporations in the U.S. He always preached lifting others up, especially the family members, and he demonstrated these teachings by providing for his mother until her demise and by looking after his brother, even in his old age.